the
search

To Wooly
Great Blessings
& love,

Nitia

The Search is a real life novel, detective story, and deep lesson that the reward for searching out a personal truth is the discovery of a universal one.

Gloria Steinem

the
search
a memoir of an adopted woman

TITIA ELLIS, PHD
Foreword by William M. Pinsof, PhD

iUniverse, Inc.
Bloomington

The Search
A Memoir of an Adopted Woman

iUniverse books may be ordered through booksellers or by contacting:

iUniverse
1663 Liberty Drive
Bloomington, IN 47403
www.iuniverse.com
1-800-Authors (1-800-288-4677)

Because of the dynamic nature of the Internet, any Web addresses or
links contained in this book may have changed since publication and
may no longer be valid. The views expressed in this work are solely those
of the author and do not necessarily reflect the views of the publisher,
and the publisher hereby disclaims any responsibility for them.

ISBN: 978-1-4502-5296-6 (sc)
ISBN: 978-1-4502-5297-3 (ebook)

Printed in the United States of America

iUniverse rev. date: 11/30/2010

For my family,
Who fill me with joy and hope.

And especially for Bill,
my soul mate and dearest companion.

In search of my mother's garden, I found my own.

—Alice Walker

The moment one definitely commits oneself, then Providence moves as well.

All sorts of things occur to help one that would never have otherwise occurred.

A stream of events issues from the decision, raising in one's favor all manner of unforeseen accidents, meetings and material assistance that no one could have dreamed would come their way. Whatever you can do or dream you can do, begin it. Boldness has genius, power, and magic in it. Begin it now.

—Goethe

This is a true story, depicting real events and real people. Some of the names and places have been changed to respect individual privacy.

Contents

Foreword

The alchemy of Titia Ellis's *The Search* astounds. She has transformed her experience of "blind" adoption and the quest to know the truth of her families (adoptive and birth) into a compelling narrative that provides hope and inspiration to anyone who has been adopted or participated in the adoption process (birth parents, adoptive parents, etc.). The tenacity of her search for her birth parents and the story of that search show how the human spirit and desire for the truth can transcend fear, in oneself and others, as well as the obstacles that a closed society places in the way of those who want to know.

Fortunately, with the advent of open adoption, the conditions and attitudes that prevailed when Titia was adopted and even began her search, are no longer as prevalent or psychologically and socially destructive. The legal, social and psychological roadblocks that she had to overcome in her quest to find her birth family and to know her truth, reflect the history of adoption in the twentieth century. The facts of that history come alive in her narrative as we search with her. Titia places the reader over her shoulder as she investigates her past. We are intimate witnesses to the hope, the despair, the frustration and ultimately the fulfillment that come her way. Reading *The Search* is like reading a mystery that grabs you and won't let go.

Although *The Search* is about an adopted person's quest to find her birth family, it is also a story about a human being's quest to know herself. Titia's courage, honesty and dogged pursuit of her past, despite the fear that surrounds such a quest, also speak to all of us, adopted or not, who desire to know the truth of where we came from and who we are. It tells us to persevere, to never lose hope and to have faith in the potential to restore shattered worlds. It shows us how the implacable quest for self-knowledge can lead us to make a better world for others. Her book is a gift that inspires and lifts the human spirit.

William M. Pinsof, PhD

The Family Institute at Northwestern University
Evanston, Illinois
July 2010

Acknowledgments

There are so many people who helped me get this book written and out into the world. It all began with Paula Hardin, precious friend and consistent support to me on every level, who invited me to join her at a writing class given by Madeleine L'Engle. It was at that seminar I discovered I loved to write. I also met Sharon Chard, who asked me to join her at a workshop with Natalie Goldberg in Taos. There I met Roberta Kern. She, Sharon, and I spent many hours writing together as I practiced saying my truth.

I attended a seminar with Deena Metzger where I met Morgan Farley. By then I knew I wanted to write the story of my search for my birth mother and asked Morgan if she would help me. Her confidence in me and her gracious teaching of the finer points of writing encouraged and enabled me to write the first draft of this book. I will be forever thankful to her for midwifing my dream into being.

I am grateful to Mikaela and Craig Barnes, dear friends and neighbors in Santa Fe, who inspired me early on by their own amazing creativity and offered their feedback along the way. My thanks go to Carl Taylor, a gentle man always filled with helpful suggestions, who put me in touch with Ruth Sylvester, a tremendous asset in assisting me to whip the first version of this book into shape.

Later I was led to Sharon Rose, a gifted editor, who helped me rise to a new level of compassion and forgiveness as I rewrote my memoir from a perspective of healing and joy. I will always be grateful for her unfailing ability to help me discover what really matters and how to convey that in the most effective way.

My deep gratitude goes to Patti Rooney, whose expertise with computers helped me send this story out while, at the same time, her humor and bright spirit made it fun. Great thanks to Liza Deignan for her invaluable wisdom and generous friendship. I also appreciate the well-honed gifts of Myra Platt and her loving support.

I am indebted to other wonderful friends who offered wisdom and encouragement along the way. Grateful thanks to Jenepher Linglebach for providing deft editing from start to finish and whose steadfast love has always blessed me on the journey. Thanks to Jen Donaldson, who turned out to be a meticulous proofreader and provider of the title All One Family, which became the name of the fund that grew out of this book. And kudos to Liz Hall, who supplied enthusiastic support and created an extraordinary bronze sculpture of an African mother and her child, which she donated to our fund.

I am most appreciative of faithful friends from the past: Patty Woerner, who played a key role in the book itself, and Marianne Johnson, both of whom were always there with wise feedback and love. Thanks also to two of my dearest friends from childhood on up, Jeanie Greene and Bettina Jenney, for the roles they played in the book as well as for always being such loyal cheerleaders. Great gratitude goes to Corson Ellis and Joan Ellis for their invaluable help at two crucial times when I was stuck during the search and for their feedback afterward.

I owe a special debt of thanks to Bill Pinsof for challenging me to make the book more transparent while at the same time believing that my story could be helpful to others. I am most appreciative of Cheryl Rampage, Ronnie Diamond, Linda Wright, and Arline Brown, for taking the time to give me valuable feedback from their professional viewpoints.

So many thanks to Susan Copeland, who has a major role in the book and now in my life. She has been a huge help when it comes to advising me in computer and Web site matters, as well as being an excellent photographer. My appreciation goes to Lesley Michaels, who offered me a different level of support through her unique gifts as a channeler. I am grateful to Audrey Arkins for her expertise in helping me with all the mechanics involved in getting a book and Web site out there, as well as for her wholehearted support. Thanks also to Spring Romer for her great help in the final stages.

There are so many others including family, friends, and clients who aided in various ways to make this a better book. Your words and lives are embedded in my heart. I wish I could name every one of you.

Thanks go to my two sons, David and Frank, for always being there for me. I am also grateful to my daughter and son-in-law, Robin and Mark Driscoll, for unexpectedly providing me with the happy ending for the book and for Robin's sage advice during the writing process. All my family have taught me so much about love.

Most of all, I am deeply indebted to my husband, who endured my long absences for more years than either of us would have guessed possible as I went through the search and then even longer as I wrote this book. The reward came as we worked more and more closely together. I can't count how many times he patiently listened to me read aloud each chapter and offered wise feedback. You are the best, Bill. I could never have gotten through this without your understanding, sound advice, and abundant love.

I cannot end without mentioning my two devoted muses, who were always present during the long hours I sat sequestered in my office. Thanks to Maya, my high spirited golden retriever, who waited so patiently by my side until I would finally get around to taking her out for a much needed run in the woods. Big hugs to Mittens, our infamously ill-tempered black cat, who slept contentedly on the rug by my feet or draped over my chair. Both left the planet just as I was nearing the end of the book, their work done, but I still feel their presence and love around me.

Introduction

As a child, I grew up feeling "less than"—mainly because I was taught early on that my being adopted was to be kept a secret, off limits for family discussion or with others out in the world. In midlife I came to see that my insecurity was a blessing in disguise for it led me on a search for my birth parents. I had to satisfy my ache to know where I belonged in the circle. This journey helped me to break through the unspoken but ever-present stigma surrounding adoption and ultimately to discover the rewards.

Along the way I learned that I needed to let go of what I wanted to have happen with both my adoptive and my birth parents and instead become open to what life had to teach me. In the process unexpected wisdom from within me and synchronistic occurrences from outside appeared to guide me. I found gifts I didn't know I was looking for including my own self, which ultimately led me to my life's true purpose.

Today it is estimated that six out of every ten people in the United States have had some sort of experience with adoption. More and more, adoption has become a "normal" way of creating a family. In addition, the rise in international adoptions is bringing in a wonderful array of children from different cultures, countries, and ethnicities. These bright and beautiful young people from all around the world are helping to lift the veil of silence that has hung over adoption for too long. At the same time, they are teaching us that we are all one family. Much to my surprise and delight, I am now privileged to be part of a family that has adopted children from abroad. Seeing how differently they are being raised from the way I was has provided the final piece of healing for me.

My years spent in searching and then writing this book have taught me that being adopted can be an invitation to find oneself, a life long opportunity that beckons to us all. For those with no genetic markers or family resemblances, the need to find out how to fit comfortably into one's skin may be more urgent. Please understand I am not suggesting that searching for one's roots is the only road to walk down or even a possibility for some who have been adopted. I only know what worked for me. The choices I made helped me become more aware of and grateful for the many gifts I have received, not only from my search but also from having been adopted in the first place. Discovering this has given me a great sense of peace and fulfillment about all that has happened in my life.

In this spirit I offer my story to those of you whose lives are touched by adoption and to all individuals and families facing the challenges that life inevitably brings. If anything I have written proves helpful, that is my joy.

— 1 —

AWAKENING

BEING ADOPTED WAS A taboo subject in our home when I was growing up. I can remember only three occasions when the topic arose. Not surprisingly, each one made a huge impact on me.

My older sister and I were our parents' precious daughters. We lived in a beautiful home in a small town outside of Chicago and had a wonderful nurse named Nonie who took care of us. When I was three and Leslie four and a half, there was great excitement in our household because my mother had a new baby who weighed only two pounds and two ounces. I waited and waited for Wally to come home from the hospital so I could play with him. When he finally arrived, he was adorable but so tiny and sick that I wasn't allowed near him. Instead my mother was always in his bedroom, and soon our beloved Nonie was also there to help. A new nurse came to take care of us, and life was never the same after that.

The greater implication of Wally's arrival into our family didn't become clear until one morning two years later when our parents called Leslie and me into their bedroom and shut the door behind us. We sat expectantly on the white couch at the end of our parents' canopied bed, thinking something exciting was in store for us. Our mother, still in her pink, silk dressing gown, sat in the chair opposite us, twisting a white lace handkerchief between her hands, while our father, in his usual blue blazer and gray flannels, paced the floor behind her.

"Girls," she started off hesitantly, "Daddy and I want to tell you something important about when you were born."

She paused for a moment and cleared her throat. My father came over and put his hand on her shoulder.

My stomach lurched. This wasn't starting off the way I had imagined.

"Now children," she said, "you know that your little brother grew in my tummy because you saw it getting bigger."

She didn't look at us as she spoke but patted her stomach instead. There was a long silence. My mother took a deep breath and started in again. "But you two didn't come out of my tummy. Daddy and I picked you out of all the little babies that didn't have parents because we wanted you for our own children."

"Why didn't we have any parents?" asked Leslie, always braver than I.

"It's a very sad story," my mother replied. "Your parents died right after you were born, so you were taken to a special house to be looked after until new parents could come for you. And that's what we did. We went all the way to New York City to find just the perfect little girls and bring them home to be part of our family."

My mother beamed at us after she said this.

"How did our mommy die?" my sister persisted.

"Actually, you each had a different mother," she said. "We're not really sure how they both died. I just know it was right after you were born."

"And our daddies?" Leslie was relentless. "What happened to them?"

I wanted her to stop. Couldn't she see the tears rolling down our mother's cheeks?

"Yes, yes, they died in this terrible accident too. But you are not to think about them anymore because now you have Daddy and me for your parents. And we love you very much."

"But what kind of accident?" Leslie wailed.

At that moment, my father stepped in front of us. "That's enough. You are making your mother unhappy."

"Yes, darlings. We never need to talk about this again, do we?" my mother said. "Come give us a hug. Then why don't you go down and ask Hilda for some of that yummy gingerbread as a little treat?"

That night as I lay clutching my white teddy bear in my bed across from Leslie, I decided not to think about those other parents ever again. I just wanted to make this mommy and daddy really happy so I would never lose them.

$*$ $*$ $*$

When I was eight, my sister informed me that our older cousin had told her that none of our parents had died after all.

"Then why didn't they want us?" I managed to ask as my heart began turning flip-flops.

"You're too young to understand."

"Did I do something bad?" By now I was crying.

"*You* didn't," she answered, looking very mysterious. "And stop being such a baby."

With that she walked off, but not before I saw that her lower lip was quivering almost as much as mine.

How I wanted to go to the mommy I had now, climb up into her arms, and ask her if all this was true. I needed her to hold me, tell me not to worry, say that she loved me. Then I would feel safe enough to ask her the question that bothered me most of all. Did she love me as much as she loved Wally, whom I had heard my aunt refer to as her "real" child?

But, of course, I didn't dare ask any of these questions because I was afraid I might make her cry. I didn't even have the nerve to try to sit on her lap. Anyway, I was scared I already knew the answer to that last one. How could she possibly love me as much as she loved my little brother, who had grown in her tummy and would have died if she had not spent his whole first year doing everything she could to keep him alive?

$*$ $*$ $*$

There was one other talk about being adopted, this time with our mother, when I was eleven and Leslie twelve. I was roller-skating one afternoon along the sidewalk outside our home when my mother drove by in her car. She stopped, opened the window, and told me to come inside right away. When I walked into the living room, my mother and sister were already there waiting for me.

Without any ado, my mother jumped in.

"Darlings," she said, "I have something important to talk with you about."

I sat up very straight, wondering what she was going to say.

"You never knew your grandfather on your father's side because he was ill when we brought you into our family, Leslie, and died before you were born, Titia. So he was not aware that your father and I adopted you two beautiful girls. As a result, you were left out of his will, which means he didn't leave you any money when he died."

I started feeling kind of sick to my stomach. I had never heard my parents discuss money before, and now my mother was talking about our being adopted as well. We knew we were never supposed to mention that topic in our family because it would upset her.

Leslie, as usual, was more on the ball. "Did our grandfather leave money to everyone else in the family?" she asked.

"Well, yes, he did," my mother replied. "The reason for that was because they were all lawful descendents, which means they were related to him by blood. Now if he'd only known what delightful children you were, even if you weren't related by blood, I'm sure he would have included you in his will."

I wondered if that were true, but all I really knew was that I didn't like hearing any of this. I just wanted to get back on my skates and go very fast down the hill.

"Anyway," my mother continued, "your father and I were just at the bank today where he signed some papers that will include both of you in his will."

She smiled at us. "So you don't have to worry. Isn't that grand?"

I smiled back at her and said, "Yes," knowing I should be feeling grateful for my father's generosity. But all I could think about was that there had to be something really wrong with us being adopted. It must mean we weren't good enough to be part of the larger family.

That was the last conversation about adoption for the next thirty years.

*   *   *

It never occurred to me as a child that I was living in a unique world because I was adopted by prominent, wealthy parents who provided me with an extraordinary amount of material privilege. I was sent to the best private schools, and our family traveled to lovely places for vacations. Since all my friends lived in the same affluent suburb in large homes, staffed by servants, and attended the same private school, I took my special position for granted, unaware that a whole other world existed outside of my bubble. Blind to my good fortune, all I cared about back then was fitting into my parents' life and being loved.

When I was twelve, my naïve point of view began to be challenged. A new girl entered our school. Bettina became one of my closest friends and has remained so ever since. How I loved going over to her house, which was in the nicest part of town, yet I was surprised to discover they had no servants. Imprinted in my heart is the memory of sitting around a table in a cozy alcove of the kitchen watching Bettina's mother, whom I adored, cooking dinner, which she served to us right at that table. What a change from my home where the cook did not welcome a curious little girl into her domain and all our meals were served to us in the dining room. My goal from then on, which I told no one because somehow it seemed disloyal to my parents, was to create that same warm scene for the family I would have when I grew up.

A year after college, I married Bill, who was a pilot in the United States Air Force and had grown up in the same small town as I had. When our first child was born, I looked down at David as he nursed at my breast and wept tears of joy. It had suddenly dawned on me that I had just produced my first blood relative. When he turned out to look a lot like me—the first person who ever had—my heart overflowed with awe and gratitude. When Robin and then Frank arrived in the next two years, my joy was complete. We had our own family, the very thing I had wanted all my life to compensate for the insecure and unlovable feelings I had experienced over being adopted.

But then life began spinning out of control. My back, which had always been a problem, collapsed, necessitating three operations in the next decade. Our marriage collapsed along with it. The simplest reason I can give for this was that neither one of us had any idea of how to discuss difficult issues in a constructive fashion. Only years later would I understand that I held myself back from being truly loving. Since I lived in fear that Bill, or anyone important to me, might leave me some day, I had to protect myself by not committing too deeply. In this way I helped create the very outcome I most dreaded. After years of struggling, we reluctantly decided to get a divorce. My sole purpose in life—to be the perfect wife and mother—had blown up in my face.

I realized I would have to tell my parents the painful truth about our marriage. This was not a happy thought as I had also attempted to be the perfect daughter. All this was complicated by the fact that Bill and I lived next door to my parents on land they had given us. Why did we ever choose to do such a thing? It's evident I still had the need to be near my mother to earn her love. That certainly would seem to qualify as yet another reason why our marriage had floundered. As for my father, I really didn't care about his opinion because our relationship had soured during my childhood.

Having called to make a morning date, I stumbled across the lawn to my parents' home, wondering how my mother was going to react and wishing just a trifle late that we had never moved into their backyard. After Lila, the maid, let me in, I walked across the black and white marble floor in the front hall and entered the spacious dining room where my mother was seated at the head of the long, mahogany table finishing a cup of coffee and reading the paper.

My mother was beautiful—soft brown hair curled around her face, framing her blue eyes and their compelling gaze, perfect complexion on which she never used any makeup except light lipstick and a dash of powder on the tip of her nose. The stylish clothes she wore accentuated her trim figure. When she saw me, she stood up to exchange the usual family greeting, an oh-so-brief kiss on the cheek. We walked across the front hall into the living room.

"We're leaving shortly to go into Chicago for lunch and the symphony," she said, straightening the skirt of her white suit. "Your father will be down soon."

She seated herself in her customary place, a comfy upholstered chair of brown and white linen next to the fireplace, and carefully crossed her legs. I sank down on the matching sofa across from her and looked around the beautiful room with its paneled wood walls and large French windows that let in the morning sunlight. I had spent so much of my childhood in this room. At this moment I was back there, feeling like a naughty little girl.

At least my father wasn't there too. I was sure I would have a better chance of being accepted and understood by my mother.

Bracing myself, I blurted out, "Mom, I have some bad news to tell you."

Her smile froze. I hurried on before I lost my nerve. The little speech I had rehearsed over and over spilled out.

"You've probably noticed that Bill and I have been unhappy in our marriage for several years. I feel horrible about it, but we are going to get a divorce."

Her reply was not what I hoped for.

"I'd heard rumors about this, but I refused to believe them. How could you consider doing such a thing?"

I had no answer for her. My main focus was on trying to quell the tears that were threatening to spill over.

My mother wasn't finished. She fixed her penetrating eyes on me.

"Do you realize we have never had a divorce in this family? I can't believe you could let yourself and all of us down by making this horrendous choice. And what about your three children? You'll ruin their lives as well, all because of your selfishness."

Hearing the disdain in her voice, I felt an unexpected anger surge through me. The last thing I needed to hear when I was at my very lowest was my mother tearing me down even further. Nor was I going to suffer the final humiliation of letting her see me fall apart. Although I felt devastated at that moment, I realize now that my mother's response was just what I needed. In that instant, it was as if the cord that had bound me inextricably to her side began to unravel.

Just then my father walked into the room.

"That's enough," he said, looking straight at my mother. "Can't you see Titia is hurting already?"

I could hardly believe what I was hearing. My father, the man who had caused me so much unhappiness in my childhood, with whom I had no real contact, was sticking up for me. What's more, he was admonishing my mother, the woman he had always deferred to and worshiped as if she were the queen.

"Thanks, Daddy," I mumbled as I rushed out of the room.

My mother and I did not speak to each other for weeks. My lifelong fear had come true. If I weren't the good daughter, my mother, who had chosen me over all those other children in need of parents, wouldn't love me anymore.

*   *   *

One month later, I sat down in the red leather chair in Bill's den clutching a little piece of paper that I'd had in my desk drawer for some time. On it was written the name and number of a divorce lawyer whom my father, my unexpected ally, had found for me. Bill had moved out, had already seen a lawyer, and was waiting for me to do the same. I had put this action off as long as I could. I made myself pick up the phone and dial. At that very moment, I had this strong knowing coming from somewhere deep inside me telling me not to call the lawyer.

Stunned, I put down the phone. This didn't make any sense. We had gone too far to turn back. Who or what was telling me this, anyway? All I knew was that it spoke with such wisdom and conviction that I, who had felt torn by self-doubt and confusion for months, knew I should listen. And the truth was, I felt relieved. Maybe we could make this work after all.

I want to say here and now to those of you who have never heard some sort of advice emerging from inside your being that this incident may sound totally implausible. I certainly wasn't going around afterward announcing to people that I had had this strange communication. But ever since that time, I have encountered this inner knowing or intuition with increasing frequency. It could happen anywhere—during my meditation or just as often when I am out taking a walk or doing the dishes. The key for me was to pay attention and trust this kind of guidance even when my logical mind tried to discount it.

*   *   *

Not long after that, Bill and I reconciled. For a while it looked as if we might succeed, but soon all the old problems resurfaced. We couldn't go on this way hurting our beloved children and ourselves. Divorce seemed like the only way out. My mother was right. I had failed everyone, including myself—whoever that was.

On a bleak, wintry morning, I was walking along the icy road down to the lake. Above me the sky was dark; a snowstorm was predicted. My body felt like a dead weight, stuffed to the brim with all the garbage of my life that I had tried so hard to suppress. In desperation, I looked up, and out of my mouth came the words, "God, if you are there, I need help."

Nothing happened. The heavens didn't part to emit a great light, no crashing thunderclouds erupted, no wild burst of snow. Nothing. Slowly I turned around and made my way home. But for the first time in months, I was more obsessed by what I had just done than over my never-ending emotional drama.

What had made me ask God for help? I had never ever thought of doing something so extreme before. For that matter, I couldn't remember asking anyone for help in my whole life. In my family, we were raised to be self-reliant. Talking about emotional problems wasn't a viable option.

Two days came and went. God was remaining ominously silent. He was probably too busy with everyone else's problems. After all, I hadn't been to church in years, so I must have been at the bottom of his list. On the other hand, maybe something was happening because I still seemed to be somewhat functional, despite the fact that just beneath the surface my whole being was engaged in a tug of war that felt like it would rip me apart.

And then in a rather roundabout way, I found what I needed. Not because I was able to admit to someone that I was in trouble and needed help. Oh, no—that certainly wasn't my style, not back then. But I did ask my friend Patty, who was in my women's singing group, if we could meet the next day to practice a tap dancing routine we were learning for a new act. Now it may sound bizarre that I was concerned about performing a silly dance step when my whole life was falling apart. But the truth was that my singing group was about all that kept me sane during that time. We had come together because we loved to sing, laugh, and perform high class numbers like "Yes, We Have No Bananas" and "There Was an Old Lady Who Swallowed a Fly" to captive audiences in nursing homes and schools.

When Patty told me she couldn't meet with me because she was going to a Bible study group, I was dumbstruck. How could my most intelligent friend be doing such a thing? I had heard these groups were springing up all around town. Yet despite the fact that I was in deep trouble, I had stubbornly resisted the idea of being with a lot of women discussing their problems and reading Bible verses.

But that voice said, "Go. After all, you *did* ask God for help."

So the following morning there I was, sitting in a stranger's living room listening uneasily to eight women talking about praying to Jesus.

9

They acted as if he were a real person who loved them and had the power to forgive and heal. I had never thought of Jesus in this way. Since college, when I had begun to question everything, including my simple childlike faith, I had stopped believing in the story of the Immaculate Conception. In my mind, Jesus was relegated to myth—an inspiring one to be sure—but just how the Bible ever became a best seller was beyond me. When one of the women declared that her whole life had changed when she had asked Jesus for guidance, I tuned her out. I could not imagine he would want to help someone who had hurt all the people she loved as I had done, especially when I didn't believe in him in the first place.

I sat through that whole two hours without saying a word, feeling like a fraud. When at last it was over, I rushed for the front door, practically falling over myself to reach the security of my car. Once safely inside, I locked the door and sat there breathing hard, trying to stifle all the feelings that were battering my insides. But it was no use. All of a sudden great sobs from the depth of my being welled up like waves, crashing through me and leaving me shaken. I couldn't stop them, nor did I even care for once about what I must have looked or sounded like to the other women who were getting into their cars around me.

When the torrent finally ceased, I mopped my face and peered cautiously out the window. No cars were in the driveway. I was all alone. And then I felt something I had never experienced in my entire life. Those anguished feelings that had been torturing me for months seemed to have been washed away. In their place was a new and amazing sensation filling me up, which I can only describe as a feeling of peace, even joy. It was so astonishing that I stayed there for a long time basking in the glow.

It just so happened that Bill and I were meeting that evening in Chicago for dinner. We had been trying to have romantic get-togethers to rekindle our marriage, but each time everything ended in disaster. That night, it all turned around. Conversation moved easily; at one point I even found myself laughing.

Finally Bill put down his fork and stared at me.

"What's going on with you?" he asked. "You're different. Maybe I am too. All I know is we haven't had an angry word between us this whole meal nor have you ended up crying."

"I feel different," I confessed. "I don't know what it's all about, but I went to a Bible study group this morning where they were all talking about prayer and healing. Afterward I went outside and cried my eyes out. Ever since, I've felt filled with this strange substance. It's sort of like laughing gas."

"You actually sound happy," Bill marveled. "Whatever has caused it, don't stop. I like you this way."

When we went to bed that night, I was terrified that I would still be that all-too-familiar stressed-out wreck when I awoke. But when morning came, I felt the same peace and joy permeating my being. For the first time, I really believed we could work out our problems after all.

I began attending the Bible groups in earnest, two different ones each week, just to make sure I was staying on track. Together with God's message of love and forgiveness, the acceptance and affirmation of those women helped me feel I actually had value. Since I had lived my whole life trying to make up for being adopted and then proceeded to make an unholy mess of everything, all this brought me hope for a fresh start.

About a month later, that same mysterious knowing directed me to give up smoking—not something I wanted to hear at all. It took three days of that message coming every time I lit another cigarette before I finally gave in and stopped, cold turkey. My reliance on the alcohol and pills I imbibed to blot out my back pain—but mostly to dull the emotional turmoil—took much longer to end, but it slowly ebbed as well. This God/inner voice business was turning out to be full of wondrous surprises, far beyond anything my limited mind could have imagined.

*   *   *

Even though I embraced my newfound spirituality with my whole heart, that didn't mean I was completely healed. Anyone could see that I still lacked some basic tools to help me navigate everyday living in more satisfying ways. I was definitely ripe for some psychological help. During a therapy session, I had one of those "aha" moments that was to change the course of my life. It started with my realization that I had always tried to please others so they wouldn't leave me. Ouch.

Where was the selfless, loving Titia I had wanted so badly to be? That image had gone hand in hand with my flailing efforts to be the perfect daughter, wife, and mother. I was sitting there trying to take in the painful fact that I had no idea who I was any longer.

From far off, I heard my therapist ask, "Titia, what do you want for yourself?"

After a long silence, out of my heart came the words, "I want to find my mother."

With that, I burst into tears.

— 2 —

THE JOURNEY BEGINS

Growing up, I had dutifully tried to push away any fantasies and feelings I had about my first mother. But my unconscious had other plans. A dream came to me one night in which this phantom mother swooped into my bedroom in a long red gown, her dark hair flowing around her, my father just behind in a black overcoat and slouch hat.

"Darling," she cried as she embraced me. "We've come to take you with us back to Russia."

I sat up with a jolt, my whole body quivering with excitement at the thought of going away with these two remarkable people, but then I remembered I had other parents now whom I loved. With that, the dream evaporated on the spot, yet the memory remained embedded in me. From then on, I was possessed by the thought that I came from Russian nobility; at other times my parents were Russian Jews, occasionally they were simple peasants.

Now that I had taken off the lid that guarded the secrets around my past, out tumbled all my questions like unruly children impatient for my attention. Why had my mother given me up? Did she ever think of me, long for me, as I realized—to my surprise—that I longed for her? Was there some relative out there who looked like me? Did I have the right to try to find her, even though it might be disloyal to my adoptive parents?

That last question was a big one. How could I betray (a strong word, but that is what it felt like) the parents who had adopted me, given me love, and showered me with so many advantages? I owed everything to these people, and I had done my very best to earn their love and approval; at least I had with my mother. I had long ago given up any hope of being close to my father, whose anger and judgments had hurt me as a child. But underlying all my efforts was the gnawing fear that somehow I was not really lovable because my first mother had given me up.

I agonized over whether my wanting to find this mother would cost me the love of the mother I had now. Was it, in reality, a radical, selfish desire? I had never heard of anyone who had done such a thing. Maybe there was an unwritten law somewhere in heaven that labeled searching for one's first parents the unpardonable sin of an ungrateful adopted daughter.

All of a sudden support for my case appeared from a most unexpected source. *Roots*, the true story of Alex Haley's search for his African ancestors who had been shipped in irons to this country during the slave trade, was being shown on television. I watched it spellbound, tears rolling down my cheeks. Alex's courage and belief in himself, in the face of all the disapproval and anger from so many people, made a deep impression upon me. If this man dared find out the truth about his past, why couldn't I?

I decided to write to the Spence-Chapin Adoption Agency in New York, tentatively asking for any information they could give me about my first mother. My knowledge of this agency, despite my parents' refusal to discuss such matters, came about years before. I was rummaging through a drawer filled with family photos and came upon a newspaper article, yellowed with age, from the *Chicago Sun-Times* Society section heralding the "miracle birth" of my brother. The story mentioned at the end that my parents already had two children who had been adopted from Spence-Chapin in New York. I had always remembered that name, although the idea of contacting them had never before crossed my mind.

Ten days later, I received a reply to my plea to learn about my past. The moment I saw the address on the envelope, my heart began to pound. Would they be dismissive of my request, saying it was not my business, or admonish me for doing something that could be hurtful to my adoptive parents? I sat at the kitchen table with the mail spread out in front of me, holding the letter. My fingers shook and my heart stuck in my throat as I tore open the envelope and pulled out two typewritten pages.

Dear Mrs. Ellis,

I am sending you some information about your natural parents, as you requested. I am sorry that distance makes a personal interview impossible, as they are so much more satisfying. Should you ever be in New York, I hope you can let me know in advance, so that you can come to the agency.

Your birth parents were both from the New England area and their parents were also New England born.

Your mother is described in the record as "rather short with a decidedly attractive manner." She attended college and held a responsible business position. She was very close to her two brothers, both college graduates, and they were very helpful to her.

Your mother met your father through a mutual friend to whom she felt very close. When this friend suddenly married, she turned to your father for comfort. Your natural father was a college graduate who worked as a civil engineer and was interested in developing new products. He was described as tall with dark hair and eyes, and he had two brothers who were also college graduates.

Although your biological parents knew that they had no basis for marriage, they did meet to discuss your future. Both felt that a home with two parents where a child would be sought was the best choice that they could make for you. Knowing that this choice would best insure your future happiness made it easier for your mother, who was a warm and loving young woman, to surrender you for adoption. From the letters in our file, your adoptive parents felt you were a "precious gift."

These facts will provide you with some basic information about your natural parents. They will probably raise many questions, which may never be answered.

I hope this letter is of some help to you, and should you want to follow it with a telephone call, I can be reached any Thursday at Spence-Chapin.

Sincerely yours,

(Mrs.) Lisa Browne
Supervisor of Adoption Department

I put down the letter. Then I picked it up and read it all over again. I couldn't believe that I had just learned so much about my "natural" or "biological parents," two new terms for me to digest. In a flash, they had stepped out of the mysterious darkness and become flesh-and-blood people. This woman, Lisa Browne, treated my daring to ask for forbidden information as a perfectly normal request. She even said I could come to the agency and talk to her in person.

I sat there for a long time. This was huge. Why didn't I feel elated over my success? I pulled myself up from the chair and, moving like a person walking in her sleep, took the letter upstairs. Once in our bedroom, I placed it in a drawer in my desk, which I then slammed shut.

That night when Bill came home, I led him up the stairs, brought out the letter, and gave it to him. "Read this."

When he had finished, he said, "There's a lot of information in this letter. Is it what you hoped for?"

"It's true," I said. "I've just learned so much about my mother, and my father too, for that matter. I'd hardly ever thought about him before."

I considered Bill's question for a moment. "I guess I'm glad I asked. Now I know what happened."

"You don't sound sure about that."

"I feel pretty unsettled," I admitted. "There's so much to take in."

I put the letter back in the drawer. "That's that. I'm going to make dinner."

Walking down the stairs, I finally realized what was bothering me. I wasn't a child created out of passion. My mind jumped to the worst possible scenario. My natural parents didn't care at all for each other. I was the result of a one-night stand, a total accident. My mother must have been glad to get rid of me. Growing in her womb, I was nothing more than a reminder of her shame over having had sex with someone she didn't love and then paying the ultimate price.

Later when we were getting ready for bed, Bill looked over at me. "You've hardly spoken a word all night. Are you okay?"

"What more is there to say?" I replied. "I was a big mistake."

"That doesn't mean your mother didn't love you. The person who wrote this letter said it was hard for her to give you up."

"How do you know? I bet they always say that."

Fighting back the tears, I climbed into bed and pulled the covers up high around me. "All right, I've done it. Now let's not talk about it anymore."

We did not discuss the letter again for two years.

∗   ∗   ∗

Despite having given up on the search for my natural mother, good things were happening in my life. Much of it, I have to admit, was due to being in therapy. I had gone from being a victim type who faltered along on my own until someone else needed something from me to being a fervent believer in the wisdom of asking for help. After all, look what had happened on my first try with God!

One of the most important things I—Little Miss People Pleaser—learned was that it might be a good thing for me to stop worrying so much about everyone else's opinions and desires. Instead, why not discover what I believed and cared about? As I dared to become more honest about my needs in my marriage, I was greatly relieved to find that Bill still loved me. In return, he found he had some requests of his own. Little by little, our marriage began improving. And I was becoming a happier person. This was such a profound change that I made a giant leap. Why couldn't I become a therapist myself and pass along all this good news to others?

Realizing that being an investment banker no longer worked for him had caused Bill to come to the same conclusion. Soon we had both enrolled in graduate school at Northwestern on the long road toward obtaining our PhDs in psychology. The more I pursued this new path, the better I felt about who I was becoming. As long as I was on a roll, maybe this would be an auspicious time to continue my search for my natural mother.

I tried out my idea on Bill as we were eating breakfast one morning.

"I'm thinking about going to see Lisa Browne at Spence-Chapin when we're in New York visiting your brother."

A look of surprise flashed over his face. "I thought you had closed that chapter. Are you sure you want to learn more? Maybe it's best to leave it alone."

"That's easy for you to say," I flared. "You already know so much about your ancestors. All I know about mine is what's written in that letter from the agency, just one and a half pages long."

I paused for breath, surprised at how strong my feelings were.

"I felt so empty at Plymouth Rock last year," I continued, "while you were telling me the names of all your forebearers who sailed over from England and landed there in the 1600s. Can you imagine how you would feel if you weren't allowed to know anything about your past?"

"How about your adoptive parents?" Bill asked. "After all, we know they came from German and English stock. Why don't you research them?"

"No, that's not the same at all. I want to find out where *I* come from, where my ancestors lived, what they looked like, how they survived out in the new world. That would help me know more about who I am. Everyone who's not adopted knows those things. Why shouldn't I have that right too?"

Listening to what was coming out of my own mouth astonished me. I decided then and there to make an appointment with Lisa before I lost my nerve.

*   *   *

When I arrived at Spence-Chapin on the designated day, waves of fright and excitement were racing each other up and down my body. Walking up the long, curved staircase, I saw a small woman with curly brown hair, dressed in a gray skirt and black sweater, waiting for me at the top.

After we introduced ourselves, I followed her down the hall and into her office, a little square room dominated by a large, wooden desk. On the desk lay a thick manila folder. Oh my heavens, that must be it—my history! My heart flew into my throat. Lisa sat down behind the desk and motioned for me to sit across from her.

"I'm glad you came," she began and pointed to the folder. "This is your file. It's been so many years since you were adopted that I had to go down into the vault in the basement to find it."

I was mesmerized by that file. It was all I could do to pull my gaze away from it and look at Lisa.

"It's taken me forty-three years to believe I had the right to find out about my mother. My adoptive mother never wanted to talk about her. I guess you could say I'm a late bloomer."

"Good for you that you've decided you can do this now," Lisa said.

I let out a long sigh. What a relief to hear her affirming the dubious action I was taking.

She put on her glasses, opened up the file, and pulled out a sheet of paper. The suspense was killing me.

"Are you ready to hear what's in this?"

I nodded, unable to speak. All my breath seemed to have been siphoned out of my chest.

"Let's see. It says your maternal grandfather owned a general store in Vermont. I like that."

"So do I," I managed to reply.

I couldn't believe it. I had just learned what state my mother came from—Vermont, of all places. My adoptive mother's family came from Vermont too. What an amazing coincidence. Or was it? Maybe their shared background was the reason I was chosen. As for the general store, back then I could only imagine that it was similar to our local hardware store. Years later I would learn that the general store was the heart of every small town in Vermont and that each one had its own special character.

Lisa read on about the details of how I came into being, but I already knew all this from her original letter. I wanted to learn something new.

My wish was granted when she suddenly said, "You were born in a hospital at 7:28 PM."

I felt chills! Knowing the exact time of my birth made me feel almost normal. A wild thought flew through my head. Now I could finally have my astrological chart done.

Lisa continued, "There was no mention of your birth mother's parents, so it seems she didn't tell them about her pregnancy. Of course, back in 1934, you must remember it was considered a terrible thing for an unmarried woman to have a baby. She probably felt a great deal of shame and guilt. That's why the original birth certificate is changed. The authorities wanted to protect the child by taking away the stigma of having ILLEGITIMATE stamped in large letters and the father listed as "Unknown" on the baby's record. Then when the child is adopted, an amended birth certificate is created, signifying a fresh start."

I hadn't known any of that. My poor mother. And who were these "authorities" anyway? I could see how creating these secrets might have made sense at one point. Yet that was all long ago. It couldn't still be such a disgrace to have a child out of wedlock. But what really made no sense at all was that this strange woman sitting across the desk from me knew more about my mother than I did. That just wasn't fair. With every fiber of my being, I wanted to grab that file and run down the stairs and out of the building with it under my arm. After all, this was *my* story. I should have the right to know every word of it. The absurdity of the situation made me feel crazy, and I lost my cool.

"Do you know my real mother's name?" I blurted out.

"No. I'm sorry, I don't," she said quietly.

"Do you at least have my original birth certificate?" My voice was getting louder, but I couldn't stop myself.

"It's not in our file," Lisa replied calmly, unfazed by my outburst. She obviously was used to dealing with people who had been adopted and became distraught when the bureaucracy blocked them from finding out the truth.

"But," she added, "I will make a further search for it." She thought for a moment. "I believe in those days the adoptive parents were given all the identifying information. It wasn't against the law in New York back then for them to have it in their possession."

"You mean my parents might have it at home?" The room seemed to start spinning, and I found myself gripping the sides of my chair. "Do I dare ask them to give it to me?"

"Well, you said you were a late bloomer," she responded lightly. "I'm sure you are ready to stand up to your mother by now."

I felt like a lightning bolt had just gone through me. This woman worked for Spence-Chapin, the official repository of the secrets of my past. Yet she was encouraging me to ask my adoptive mother for the document that contained my natural mother's name. Maybe she was on my side after all.

As if she had read my mind, Lisa began talking about how frustrating it must be for me to know this much and no more. Little did they realize back in the 1930s and 1940s when the social workers were trying so hard to protect the baby, the birth parents, and the adoptive parents that one day the adoptee would begin to question this whole procedure of secrecy and demand to know the truth. Lisa was hopeful that the laws would be changed at some point, but it would be too late to help people my age.

One of the most interesting and unusual things about my adoption, Lisa added, was the large amount of correspondence that went back and forth between my adoptive mother and a Mrs. Greer, who was a board member of Spence-Chapin at that time. She said my adoptive father was always in the background, a shadowy figure, while my mother emerged through these letters as a very powerful woman who threatened to withhold her charitable contributions if the agency didn't do what she wanted.

Lisa looked down at the file. "Did you know that your sister was here as well? She came in years ago when the original executive director was still here."

All of a sudden I had a vague recollection of Leslie mentioning something about visiting Spence once with a cousin. So I wasn't the only one who wanted to know the truth after all! That thought gave me great comfort.

"Does she know you are here now?" Lisa asked.

"Leslie died last year from a medical condition," I replied, unable to keep my voice even.

"I'm so sorry," Lisa murmured. "She must have been awfully young."

"Yes, just forty-two. She left four children, the youngest only seven. I miss her terribly. I think I'm doing this for both of us, even though I know we had different mothers."

"Were you two very close?" Lisa asked.

I thought about her question for a moment. Leslie and I were so different from each other. Although she was only a year and a half older, she seemed light-years ahead of me with her tall, willowy body, striking red hair, green eyes, a dramatic flair in clothes and in temperament. I, on the other hand, with my nondescript brown hair and eyes and medium build, seemed the total opposite, more comfortable playing out in the ravine with my pals than flirting with boys, and definitely the good middle child wanting to make sure the waters were never ruffled. As a result, when Leslie stood up to our mother—the only one in our family who had the courage to do such a thing—I rushed in to protect my mother. Not surprisingly this created a wedge between us, but back then I felt I had to choose sides, and I needed my mother most of all.

"I wish we could have been closer as children," I said, shaking my head and pulling myself out of the myriad of memories washing through me.

"Yet despite our differences, there was a real bond between us. When we each got married, I was her maid of honor, and she my matron of honor. We also chose each other to be the godmother of our firstborn. And I will always be grateful for Leslie's earthy side because it was she who encouraged me to try natural childbirth and breast-feed my babies, neither of which was in vogue back in the late fifties and early sixties. It meant the world for me to nurse my own children."

I stopped as a new thought came to me. "I wonder if my birth mother ever nursed me."

"I'm afraid I don't have the answer to that," Lisa replied.

My heart ached. It would have meant so much to know if she had done that.

"And you," Lisa asked, "how has your life turned out?"

"I guess I always feared that my adoptive mother must love my younger brother more than she did me," I said. "He was their real son and heir, the child she had been told she could never have. I wanted to ask her if she loved me as much as him, but I never did, probably because I was afraid of what she'd say."

"I imagine most adoptees whose parents also have natural-born children must have the same questions," Lisa said. "If they don't feel safe talking about all that with their parents, their concerns go underground and get bigger."

"On the other hand," I added, "Wally and I were much more alike and had a lot of fun together when we were young. I remember the year the Cubs won the pennant, and we followed their whole season and knew all the statistics for each player. Although he married and moved away years ago, I know my family and I can always count on him if we ever need anything. And I am there in the same way for him."

"And what about your father?" Lisa asked. "You haven't said anything about him, the man in the shadows."

"We didn't have a good relationship," I admitted. "I was scared of him."

Then I remembered how my father stuck up for me when my marriage was falling apart and surprised myself by saying, "Maybe that will change someday."

I told Lisa about giving birth to three children whom I cherished and how my back fell apart after that. We had always wanted to have five kids, so Bill suggested we adopt, but I refused point blank. I could never bring an adopted child into our family when we already had three biological children, not after my own experience.

I knew our time was running short, so I made my final plea. "I am here today because if I can find my birth mother, maybe the hole that has been inside me all my life will be filled."

"That's what so many adoptees believe will happen once they find her," Lisa sighed. "I have to tell you that it's so often unsatisfying for people even when they do find out who their natural parents are. They think all they need to do is just see them once or talk to them briefly. But they haven't counted on all the emotions that come into play. And, of course, sometimes the people they discover don't want to be found. Most of them have gone on with their lives and never told anyone their secret. Or they weren't very nice to begin with. They also could be in bad straits or ill and want money from their child or the adoptive parents."

I didn't want to hear her say any of those things. None of this would be true about my mother.

"And there's the other part," Lisa added as we walked down the hall, "the vulnerability of the adoptive parents. They are always scared their child will find out who their natural parents are and then not love them anymore."

Was she trying to discourage me from searching further by telling me this? She didn't know my adoptive mother, that "powerful" woman so accomplished and strong. Of all people, she wouldn't be threatened by what I was doing.

How little I knew back then. Perhaps that was a good thing.

No matter what Lisa says, I thought as I walked slowly down the stairs, I have the right to look for my first mother.

— 3 —

REVERBERATIONS

AFTER MY VISIT TO Spence-Chapin, I felt empowered and ready to move forward with my search. I wrote Lisa, thanking her for her kindness and for her offer to help me obtain my original birth certificate. A few weeks later she sent me my amended one, saying that the original was not in their files. Reading it, I was disappointed to find that the only new information beyond the obvious facts that I was female and born in Manhattan was the name of the hospital where I was born. My adoptive parents' names had been substituted for my birth parents'. Who would have guessed back then that this seemingly useless piece of paper would end up being the key to unlocking the door to my past?

But that was all down the road. Back then I realized my only option would be to talk to my adoptive parents to see if they had my original birth certificate. This was not a discussion I looked forward to. Did I dare risk losing the love of the only mother I had ever known because of my need to find my other mother who might not want to see me anyway? I could end up with no mother at all.

I grappled with all my doubts for weeks. Finally it came to me that it was time to have a heart-to-heart with God. Would he still care about me, I wondered, feeling a slight twinge of guilt because I had stopped going to Bible studies and hadn't spent much time praying either. But then I remembered that when I first asked for help, I was definitely a nonbeliever, and in spite of that, God had given me the opportunity to choose a new life. That thought gave me hope that he wouldn't mind my having drifted away.

So I sat down and started out rather awkwardly. "God, I'm sorry I haven't talked to you in such a long time. Hopefully, we are still friends. If that is true, I have a problem that I need your help with. I want to know who my biological mother is. Can you tell me if it's all right to keep looking for her even though others—well, let's be honest, I'm talking about my adoptive mother here—may not like it?"

I waited, determined not to get up until I had my answer. Probably I fell asleep. Whatever happened, when I came to, I felt at peace, a feeling I hadn't experienced in a long time. Maybe this was my sign. Before God or I could change our minds, I picked up the phone and invited my mother over for tea that afternoon. Knowing how busy her life was, I suspected she wouldn't be able to fit me into her schedule. Much to my surprise, she said she could come.

When my mother arrived, I took her into the living room.

"Just make yourself comfortable," I said, trying to sound calm. "I'll bring us some tea."

Oh, I was so nervous. The cups clattered all over the tray as I carried them in. At least I had invited her over to my house, where I felt just a bit more powerful being on my own turf.

My mother was edgy too; not being in control was definitely out of her comfort zone. She talked about all sorts of inconsequential things. Usually I hung on her every word. Today it was different.

Saying a silent prayer, I plunged in. "Mom, I invited you over because I want to talk with you about my being adopted. I need to know more about where I came from."

My mother's face transformed before my eyes into an opaque mask.

I had blown it. Why did I have to hit her with that in the first sentence?

"And just what is it you want to know?" she asked icily, fishing in the pocket of her dress for her handkerchief.

"Now, Mom, please don't worry." I backtracked hastily. "You are my mother, and I love you very much."

The lines around her mouth softened slightly.

"Well, I love you very much too," she said stiffly, "always have, ever since the day your father and I saw you lying in your crib at Spence and knew you were the baby we wanted."

"Tell me about that," I begged. This was the first time she had ever talked to me about the details of my adoption. I was hungry for every word.

"There's really nothing more to say. We took you home on the train the next day. Then we had to come back with you six months later to go to court to make the adoption official."

I could have used a warm, fuzzy description here, like *we were so in love with this adorable little baby girl whom we had yearned to have for so long* but that was not my mother's style.

I shook off my fantasy and said, "How fascinating. I never knew that before."

"Well, you could have asked me," she said irritably.

"No, Mom, it was impossible to ask you anything about my adoption. I knew you would cry if I did. I didn't want to make you sad."

"Of course I didn't want to talk to you and Leslie about your being adopted," she replied. "The whole point was to forget all about your past. You were our beloved children. We did everything we could to make you feel part of our family."

She was starting to choke up. I had to speak fast.

"I know that, and I appreciate all you've done for me. But that doesn't take away my yearning to know where I come from. Not having any information about the generations that lived before me makes me feel as if I'm some kind of alien from outer space."

I gulped and took a deep breath. "And you might as well know that I have been in correspondence with a social worker at Spence-Chapin. If only for medical reasons, I need to know about my birth parents. The woman who responded invited me to come and see her, so I went when we were in New York this winter. It was wonderful to talk with her and learn some things about my past, but she wasn't allowed to tell me my birth mother's name or any other identifying information."

There, I had said it. My heart was beating so fast I thought it would burst out of my chest. When I dared to look over at my mother, she seemed to be in a state of shock. I had never seen her at a loss for words.

"Are you okay?" I asked nervously.

Her face crumpled as if I had smashed her with my fist. A tear ran down her cheek.

Determined not to let her melt my resolve, I continued, "Please remember that I love you. This has nothing to do with that. But I have to know more about my other mother."

My mother sighed heavily and wiped her eyes. "All right," she said with resignation. "If it really means so much to you to know more, I will go to New York and talk to the people at the agency. They will certainly tell me about your birth parents."

Now it was I who was shocked. I couldn't believe she was saying this. "That is the most generous, loving act you could ever do for me."

I leaned over and threw my arms around her. I could feel her heart pounding wildly. Oh, no, had I caused that? Was she going to have a heart attack right here on my living room couch?

My mother carefully disentangled herself from my embrace, stood up gingerly, and straightened her dress. "I have to run," she announced. "We're having people for dinner tonight."

I stood up too. "Thank you so much for coming over and for offering to find out more information for me. I know it's not an easy thing for you to do."

"No, it certainly isn't," she retorted. "Never in my wildest dreams did I imagine you would ask this of me."

She thought for a moment. "This whole notion of yours must be due to all that psychotherapy you've been having."

I smiled somewhat sheepishly. "Therapy certainly has helped."

"I thought so," she said triumphantly.

Brushing my cheek with her lips, she pulled on her coat and sailed out the door.

∗   ∗   ∗

The dance began. After hearing not a word from my mother for weeks, I phoned to remind her of her promise. She countered, saying she was too busy to go to New York. I urged her just to call them up and ask for the information. More weeks went by. I called again, upping the ante this time by asking if she would look for my original birth certificate since Spence-Chapin didn't have it in their files. It was a big request since we both knew full well that was the document that contained the name of my biological mother. My mother replied firmly, "No, we don't have it."

Finally, a few weeks later, she telephoned to say that Spence-Chapin had sent her the information I had requested. When I read their letter, I was dismayed to see it contained the same old information with only one addition—that my natural parents were in good health. I called her again to ask for the birth certificate. My mother was exasperated.

"Will you never be satisfied? Do you have any idea how awful this whole thing has been for me? Don't you care at all about my feelings?"

"You know I care, Mom. But I have feelings too. Aren't mine important?"

There was a long silence on the other end of the phone. I stopped breathing.

"I can't talk anymore," she said. "I'm late as it is."

By now I was desperate, so desperate, in fact, that the only course I could see left for me was to ask my father for help. Yes, I was going to beg a favor from the man with whom I hadn't had a real conversation in years. We met for a very uncomfortable lunch where I pleaded my case, saying they must have my birth certificate somewhere, and could he look for it because this meant so much to me. By the end of that meal, which probably gave both of us indigestion, he reluctantly agreed to do what he could.

I returned home feeling cautiously optimistic. After all, my father had astounded me once before by taking my side when my mother was berating me for causing our marriage to fall apart. Maybe he would come through for me again. When I told Bill about our meeting, even he was hopeful.

Lying in bed that night, we talked excitedly about what this might mean. By now, my husband had become my true ally. I was touched by his eagerness to help me find the truth.

I waited expectantly the next few days for my father to phone, my mind racing ahead to what I would do once I saw my mother's name on the birth certificate. I couldn't just call her up out of the blue and announce that I was her daughter. It would be wiser to write her a letter first and send a picture of our family, maybe that photo of all of us sitting on the dock up in Canada. That way she would have some time to get used to the idea that the baby she had given up over forty years ago had finally found her.

When three days passed with no word, I was almost jumping out of my skin. Looking out the kitchen window that morning, I saw Mario, my parents' gardener, walking across the lawn with an envelope in his hand. I rushed out the door to greet him.

"Hi, Titia, here's something from your mama," he said in his thick Italian accent.

"Thanks, Mario," I said as I grabbed the envelope, noting with satisfaction how thick it was. I ran up the stairs to my bedroom, sank into my chair, and ripped it open. First, I pulled out an official document, gazed at it quickly, and then threw it down on the floor. It was my amended birth certificate, not the original I had asked for. This was a bad omen. I unfolded several pages filled with my mother's distinctive slanted handwriting, already knowing I was not going to like what she had to say.

> *Darling Titia,*
>
> *This letter has to do with the birth certificate, which you have recently been requesting. I can't deny that I wish it didn't mean so much to you—for all of the reasons that we've gone into in our last two or three conversations. As you believe in absolute honesty, I can only say that the recent revelations have been just plain hell to a mother who has loved you with all her heart—as totally and equally as I have loved Wally and Leslie. The slightest thought of any differences of feeling toward any of you is impossible for me— absolutely impossible.*
>
> *I finally realized that something that you had presented to me as a perfectly logical and legitimate request to find out as much as possible about your social and medical history was, in addition, a request to find out how you could get into communication with another mother—the woman that bore you.*

When I made up my mind to go down to Spence for this information, it was like sending me down to the firing squad.

As you know, I didn't have to go as they said they would send your dossier. I gave you what they sent. But when it arrived, I realized you would be disappointed, so I called again and asked specifically about the birth certificate. Frankly, 43 and 45 years later, I didn't even remember receiving any documents but yours and Leslie's histories, which I remember they asked us to read and consider before we saw you, and then we could return them. The other document I remember being given to us was in the New York Surrogate Court over six months later when we took you east for the legal adoption proceedings (you had to be present in court with us), and then we were given your amended birth certificate, proving you were our child. Daddy's recollection is just the same as mine. These birth certificates were the all-important documents, as they proved your American citizenship, enabled you to get a passport, and all of the other things for which one needs proof of one's American birth. When you were minors, Daddy used them for your passports and has always kept them with mine—for easy accessibility on the top layer of papers in his safety deposit vault at the bank. You could have had it any time you wanted it—it just remained there for safekeeping. I enclose it here. It seems far more sensible and proper for you to have it than us.

In the second conversation with Mrs. Capel, she said we must have been given original birth certificates too, and that we must still have them as they do not have them at Spence. She said that most adoptive parents leave them there for safekeeping but we must have taken yours with us.

So Thursday Daddy and I went together into the safety deposit vault at our bank in Chicago. I don't think I've ever been in it before and Daddy says he puts something in there about once every two or three years. At the very bottom, in the back of the box were two envelopes sealed with sealing wax. These were the original birth certificates, yours and Leslie's, which I can only guess that we unconsciously relegated to our subconscious—to make you our own babies, which you have been in our minds and hearts ever since. So I called Mrs. Capel to tell her we had found them, and said, "I suppose I'll have to give Titia hers now."

This wise and admirably calm lady practically hit the ceiling. "That is impossible. You would be violating the laws of New York State which guarantee the natural mother's right to privacy and anonymity, safeguard the child's security and rights as a full member of his or her family of adoption, and protect the adoptive parents against the burden of anxiety that open records would obviously create. As you remember," Mrs. Capel continued, "at the time of adoption the original birth certificate is sealed and permanently impounded by the Surrogate Court, and an amended certificate in the child's new name is issued. Adoptions in New York State are granted on the guarantees to all parties and by all parties, of complete confidentiality."

Mrs. Capel went on to say that Spence adoptions are made on the same basis. The reason they have had such an outstanding record and reputation over the years is that they have guaranteed complete confidentiality both to the natural mother, who is the first to request it and comes to them because she knows they are trustworthy, and to the adoptive parents, who give their promise of confidentiality in return. "You would not only be violating New York State's laws but also yours and your husband's given word to Spence."

I told her that Daddy and I understood all this and neither of us would consider breaking a law, much less betraying a promise, but that I didn't know how to handle the matter of the birth certificate at this point, with you feeling so strongly. She said, "Send the

*certificates to us as so many parents have done. It is
somewhat surprising that you have them. We will keep
them safely and if the law is ever changed and your
daughter still wants hers, it will be here for her even if
you are no longer living."*

*So with a prayer in our hearts that we were doing
the only thing that we could rightly do, we took both
certificates to the Chicago post office and sent them
registered mail to Spence. I wish that we had done this
years ago, but I can only say that you and Leslie have
always been so completely our own beloved children
that we had long since forgotten that these certificates
even existed.*

*I pray that you will realize the soul searching and
heartache this decision has cost us and will agree with
us that it was the right one under all the circumstances.
Certainly for Daddy and me, the miracles of your
and Leslie's adoptions and Wally's birth and survival
are the most beautiful manifestations of God's great
goodness.*

All my love always,

Mummie

The battle was over. My mother had won! She had my original
birth certificate in her hands and she had sent it back. I felt like I had
received a major blow to my body.

It was craziness to have thought I could prevail against my mother
on this most critical issue. Lisa's last warning about the vulnerability of
adoptive parents flashed through my mind. I had not wanted to listen. I
could not believe my mother was so insecure that she feared she would
lose me to the other mother. My God, didn't she realize I had spent my
entire life trying to get her to love me?

Just thinking of Lisa made me feel better. She was the one who had
encouraged me to do this. Maybe she could help me now. I pulled myself
out of the chair and stumbled over to my desk. Shuffling through the
drawer, I found her phone number. When I dialed, I got a recording,

but just hearing her voice was comforting. I left her a message saying I was in a crisis in my search and to please call.

All I really wanted to do was to get into bed and sleep, but I knew from past experience that would only make me more miserable. Instead I forced myself to walk downstairs, call Cola, our black lab, who was sleeping in a patch of sunlight under the window, and go out the back door.

A brisk breeze was blowing, clearing away the humidity of the morning. Although I felt so weak that I could hardly navigate, I willed myself to walk behind the house into the trees and out to the bridge that crossed over the ravine running behind my parents' and our property. A few blocks down the road, I came to the top of the bluff overlooking Lake Michigan. Sitting down on the grass, I stared in a stupor at the roiling waters. Far off a sailboat was being tossed along over the waves. It looked so helpless out there, totally at the mercy of vast forces. I watched until it disappeared over the horizon. Dragging myself home, I felt as if I had just witnessed a metaphor of my life.

Shortly after I returned, Lisa called. I told her what my mother had done and then pleaded, "Can you help me?"

"Oh, my dear," she replied, "it's too late. I can't stop them from putting your birth certificate back into your file in the vault. Who was the person that told your mother she should do that?"

"A Mrs. Capel."

"Good Lord, she's only the secretary at the agency. She has no right to be telling people what they should do. I hear she's meddled that way before."

I was shocked. "How can this be? What can I do now?"

"Well, I imagine you must have a few things you want to say to your mother," Lisa said.

Her words shook me up. I had been wallowing long enough in my pain. "You're right, I do. But is nothing going to get that birth certificate back, Lisa?"

"I'm afraid not. I am awfully sorry. Call me if you need anything more. And remember, you did your best. Maybe it's time just to let it go."

Hanging up, I felt a surge of energy pour through my body. Without a second thought, I marched over the lawn to my parents' home and went in the back door. Finding Mary, the cook, chopping vegetables in the kitchen, I asked her if my mother was around.

"Yes, she just went up to her study."

Good. I was in luck. I climbed the circular staircase two steps at a time, strode through the white hallway, and burst into the room without knocking. Glancing over at the painting of my sister as a child above the fireplace, it crossed my mind how this used to be her room, the scene of many conflicts. *I could use some of your grit right now, Leslie*, I thought.

My mother was sitting with her back to the door at her massive mahogany desk, which was strewn with pads of yellow legal paper. She spun around as if she had been waiting for this encounter, her face grim.

"How could you have done it?" I demanded.

"What do you mean?"

"You know what I mean. How could you have gotten rid of my original birth certificate when you knew how much it meant to me?"

"Now, Titia, I was only doing what I had to."

"That's not true." My voice was rising. I didn't care. "There was no need to do what that woman said. And, by the way, I checked with the agency. Your 'admirably calm and wise Mrs. Capel' was nothing more than a secretary there. She had no authority to tell you anything."

A surprised look passed across my mother's face. Composing herself, she rose and stood with her hands on the back of the brown leather chair, facing me.

"What could I do?" she asked. "It was against the law to give it to you."

"The hell with the law."

Blood pounded in the vein in my neck. This was the first time in my life I, the good daughter, had ever confronted my mother, and the stakes were high—too high.

"My birth certificate was given to you when you adopted me. You weren't bound by any law. Couldn't you have thought just once about what I wanted? You sent back the one piece of information that would have told me who my birth mother was. Now it's sealed away down in the vault at Spence-Chapin forever. I'll never have a chance to find out where I came from. Are you happy about that?"

Tears welled in my mother's eyes. "Darling, we just did what we thought was best. I pray some day you will understand."

"Don't talk to me about praying. What's more, I was furious that you didn't even have the courtesy to tell me to my face what you had done. You had to send Mario over with your letter. That was the last straw."

My anger, stored up for years, was no doubt directed at both of my mothers: at my birth mother for abandoning me, and at my adoptive mother for not showing her love the way I needed her to. But I was unaware of any of that at this moment.

Pulling myself together, I shot my final arrow. "If you'd really loved me, you would have done what I asked."

It hit home. My mother looked stricken; her face withered and turned gray in front of my eyes. She started to speak but stopped and put a hand over her heart.

"That's all I have to say." I turned on my heel and left.

Walking back across the lawn, my legs shook so badly I wasn't sure I could make it. The tempest that had raged through me had moved on, sucking off all my energy. I collapsed onto a porch chair outside our home. My head was spinning. What had I done? This was the first time in my life I had yelled at my mother. I could still see the way her hand was clutching her breast when I left the room. Did that mean she was having chest pains?

I suddenly remembered that she had already had a heart attack a few years earlier just after she and my father had returned from a long trip to China. I had helped care for her so tenderly back then until she was out of danger.

Oh, my God, what if now I had killed her? I had to go back over there before it was too late and say I was sorry. How could I have been so furious? I loved my mother.

Another voice pushed its way into my mind. *Don't go over there and apologize. You did the right thing. If you take back your words, you won't be able to live with yourself. And be honest: being that powerful woman felt good.* Now that was an unexpected thought to pop up in the middle of all my angst. I hoped I could hang on to it for future reference.

Drops of rain began falling. I pulled myself out of the chair and went into the house. Collapsing on the couch in the family room, I stared into space, waiting for the phone to ring to tell me my mother had been rushed to the hospital. Should I call and ask Mary to check on her? But what if my mother answered the phone? What would I say? Despite all my confusion, I knew I was not ready to apologize. Finally I couldn't deal with it any longer. I went upstairs and gave in to the sanctuary of my bed.

When Bill came home, he found me curled up in a fetal position under the covers. "What's happened?"

I pointed to my mother's letter lying on the bedside table. Watching him read it, I felt gratified by his evident anger. After he came to the end, he exploded. "I can't believe she did that! Your mother has always managed to get her own way, but now she has completely betrayed you."

Betrayed—yes, that was the word. It conveyed my feelings exactly.

"Have you talked to her?" he asked. "I would have really given her a piece of my mind."

"I'm afraid I did more than that," I said, bursting into tears.

I told him about getting so angry that I blew up at her.

"Good for you," Bill replied, "She deserved it. It's about time someone stood up to your mother. I'm proud of you."

"But maybe the shock of it has killed her," I sobbed. "When I left, she looked deathly ill, the way she did after she had that heart attack. I've been waiting all afternoon for someone to call and tell me she keeled over."

"Don't worry. She's stronger than any of us thinks," he consoled me.

If only I could believe him. Sleep was out of the question that night as I tossed and turned, ravaged by horrible dreams filled with images of my mother being carried out inert on the stretcher, then raising her head and cursing me just before disappearing into the ambulance. At long last I watched dawn appear over the horizon. Weak with relief that there had been no frantic call from the big white house next door, I rolled over in bed and finally relaxed. She had survived my outburst. Thank God, I hadn't killed her and lost two mothers all in one day.

— 4 —

UNEXPECTED HELP

AFTER THE BIG BLOW-UP, my mother and I didn't speak to each other for a month. True to our family tradition, when we finally talked there was no mention of what had transpired between us. Our conversations from then on were polite and superficial, our meetings infrequent. Over the next two years, I concentrated on my studies at graduate school, plus the new therapy practice Bill and I were building.

I tried to forget about finding my birth mother and to ignore the rift with my adoptive mother, but other events pushed me to deal with these problems. That fall I entered the Family Institute of Chicago to receive training in my chosen field as—no big surprise—a marital and family therapist. As fate would have it, one of my first assignments was to fill out my family tree in preparation for having my clients do the same.

Then we received an invitation to the wedding of one of Bill's nieces, which was going to be held in, of all places, Vermont.

"The wedding might be in my birth mother's home town. I could pass her on the street and never even know it," I moaned to Bill.

When he asked if I'd rather not go, I quickly changed my tune.

"Vermont is my heritage. I'd at least better take a look at this state."

A week later, one of my mother's closest friends died. Sitting in the church at the memorial service, I spied my mother a few pews away looking downcast and pale. If this were her funeral and we hadn't reconciled, I would never forgive myself.

It was obvious the universe was giving me a message here. I needed to address the impasse with both my mothers, but I felt stuck. I decided to talk with Patty, the friend who had told me about the Bible study years ago and who just happened to be in the same program with me at Northwestern. We arranged to meet for lunch the next day in one of the student hangouts on campus. After we slid into a booth in the back of the room, I told her how I had been depressed ever since my mother sent back my original birth certificate. Now I wanted to start searching again, but I felt paralyzed.

My friend didn't mince words. "I know you are still angry at your mother, but I think you are just as angry at yourself for giving up all your power to her. In order not to feel that anger, you've turned it in on yourself and become depressed."

I sat back startled. "That's quite an insight."

"And anyway," Patty continued, "you have the right to keep looking for your birth mother with or without your adoptive mother's approval. This is your search, and you don't need your mother's help."

"It is my search." I felt stronger just saying that. "I know she's never going to be supportive about my doing it. I have to give up trying to please her once and for all. I am also realizing that I have been polarizing all this in my mind. It's as if I have to be angry with my adoptive mother for what she did to be able to justify looking for my other mother. That's crazy."

Driving home that afternoon, I kept saying to myself, *I can do this on my own. I know I can.* Stopping at our local bookstore to pick up a present for a friend, I idly cased the self-help section as I waited for the book to be wrapped. A paperback seemed to jump off the shelf into my hands. I looked at the title and gasped. It was called *The Search for Anna Fisher*, by Florence Fisher. Below was printed in bold, black letters:

The book that made the adoption issue hot—
the true story of one woman's efforts
to unlock the secret of her birth.

Good heavens, how astounding! When I opened it, the first thing that caught my eye was a quote by an adoptee: "I'm sure you can understand wanting to see someone in this world who is actually flesh and blood related to me."

My heart started to pound. This book was written for people like me. Imagine finding it on this particular day. It was as if some invisible benevolent hand was leading me.

Back home, I dumped all my schoolbooks and packages onto the kitchen table, made myself a cup of tea, sat down, and opened the book. I read all the way through without stopping, riveted by Florence's courage and perseverance in the face of her adoptive parents' and the bureaucracy's opposition to her search. For twenty years she looked for her birth parents (Twenty years! Oh please, God, don't let it take me that long!), going through phone books, knocking on apartment doors, being rejected over and over. When she finally found her birth mother, their reunion was not what she had hoped for. Her mother had never told her new family about Florence. Terrified that they would shun her if they knew the truth about her past, she decided not to have any more contact with Florence, her first-born child.

I couldn't let myself take this part in. It was too devastating. What if my own birth mother felt that way about me when I found her? Anna Fisher rejected her daughter, in part, because she feared publicity. By then, Florence had become well known because she had founded an organization called ALMA to support both adoptees who wanted to search for their birth parents and birth parents searching for the children they had given up.

That reminded me that someone had mentioned there was an adoptees' support group called Yesterday's Children in a town nearby. I rushed to the phone book, found the name, and called, only to hear a recording saying the office was closed. I left my name and number, but no one called me back. After waiting for two days, I called and left another message. Still no reply.

My moods were volatile. I had been excited and hopeful upon finishing Florence's book and calling Yesterday's Children. When no one responded, I felt dejected. Fearful of sinking back into the depression that always hovered over me, I had to do something to save myself, but what?

Heaven knows I had tried in oh-so-many ways to escape dealing with my depression in the past. Let's see, there was the aimless wandering in malls gazing mindlessly at things I didn't need; excessive reliance on alcohol, prescription drugs, and cigarettes; running around trying to save others while in denial that my own life was going down the tube; and when none of the above worked, the old collapsing-in-bed routine to lose myself in sleep. Obviously, in the long run, these efforts had not done the trick. They only made me feel worse about myself.

But then I reminded myself that I had chosen a different path to walk these days. I went up to my bedroom, sat down in my chair, closed my eyes, and began to pray for guidance. After telling God all of my endless problems, I finally stopped talking and tried to listen. I have to admit this was not one of my strong suits, especially when I was feeling under pressure, but listening was a skill I was trying to cultivate.

After what seemed like a long time, an answer actually came to me. I needed to have an honest talk with my adoptive mother. Of course, that made perfect sense. But this time I was not going to give up my power by asking for her approval or her help. With that clear, I phoned and asked my mother if she could come over today because I had something important to discuss with her.

A long pause ensued.

"I'm busy writing my book," she replied stiffly. "But if this is so urgent, I will try to get over in an hour."

Four hours later, she arrived.

"It took longer than I thought," she started off. "My research assistant was there, and we had many crucial things to go over."

My mother was writing a book about volunteers in politics, a subject she was an expert on, having worked on numerous candidates' campaigns. I fought off my usual tendency to ask how it was coming. We would never get to my needs if I derailed the conversation in that way.

"Well, you are here now," I began matter-of-factly, trying to ignore the anxiety pulsating through my body. "I asked you over because I want to talk to you about our relationship."

"Oh." She drew back. "What does that mean? Another one of your psychological terms?"

I wasn't going to let her hook me. "Maybe it is. I just know we haven't been close ever since the fight two years ago over my original birth certificate. I still feel angry about it being down in the vault at Spence where I can never get it again. Even though I told you how upset I was, it's not over."

I looked over at her implacable countenance and hurried on. "I don't want there to be this anger and hurt between us. It's bad for us both. I'm hoping that if we talk about this, we can get through it."

I paused, totally at a loss as to what to say next. In the past, I would have rushed to reassure her that I loved her, that everything would be all right, but I couldn't say that to her now. Silence thickened around us.

My mother cleared her throat. "Well, I have to tell you, since you are into total honesty these days, that you have hurt me terribly by all you have told me these last few years."

Her response was not what I had expected, but I had initiated this so now I had better listen.

"Please tell me what I've said that's been so painful for you."

"How can you even ask that?" she responded. "The way you told me that your childhood wasn't always a happy one. I thought you had an ideal childhood. You certainly looked happy."

She stared at me accusingly, as if I had made that up.

I didn't remember telling her I wasn't always happy as a child, but I must have admitted it at some point.

"On top of that," my mother continued, "you tell me you want to go find your real mother. How am I supposed to feel upon hearing those words? It's been absolute hell for me." She looked as though she was going to cry.

I jumped in before that happened. "I'm sorry that you have been suffering. It wasn't my intention to link the fact that my childhood wasn't always happy to my need to search for my birth mother. Whose childhood is idyllic anyway? And she is not my real mother. She's my birth mother. There's a big difference. You are my real mother, the one who raised me."

"Well," she sniffed into her handkerchief, "I'm glad to know you feel that way."

"I do. But," I went on, "I am still going to continue searching for her. I wish I could help you understand why this is so important to me. It just isn't fair that other people made a decision before I was born that I would never have the right to know where I came from. Everyone else accepts as a matter of course that they know their parents and their ancestral line, as well as whom they look like and take after. I am not allowed to know any of that. I am an adult now, not a little baby. I have the right to the truth. It has nothing to do with my feelings for you or what my childhood was like. It's about who I am."

Now it was out there between us. I sat back and tried to remember to breathe as I awaited her response.

My mother was quiet for a long time, head down, twisting her handkerchief between her fingers. Then she sighed as if some inner decision had been made, straightened up, and looked me in the eye.

"I don't like hearing what you plan to do. I wish with all my heart that you would give up this search. But if you have been thinking about it all this time, over two years, you must want to do it very badly."

My jaw dropped. My mother had actually made her way inside me to comprehend what I was feeling. I couldn't remember that ever happening before.

She offered once again to write to Spence and try to get more information for me. This time I politely but firmly turned her down.

She slumped back in her chair. Her last card had been played and rejected. Then she pulled herself up again.

"Even though I am not at all happy about this, I guess I can't change your mind. There is one favor, though, that I would ask. I would like you to keep me informed as you go along. Tell me whatever you find out."

A shiver ran through me. Speaking the truth to her about this subject that was incredibly charged between us would not be easy. On the other hand, she had made the effort to understand how strong my need to know was. I owed her this, so I agreed.

When my mother rose to leave, I noticed with concern how frail she looked. Had she been losing weight? I stood up, reached over, and took her hand. It felt cold.

Without knowing what I meant, I said, "Don't worry, Mom. This isn't the disaster you think it is. I have a strange feeling it might even bring us closer to each other. In fact, it already has."

"Well, it's comforting you think that," she laughed nervously.

I told her how much I loved her. To my amazement, I found it was true. My anger had been transformed.

Accompanying her outside and watching her walk home, her erect back receding behind the garden gate, I felt giddy with relief and joy. It was over, those two years of estrangement. My mother and I had just had an honest conversation about the most problematic issue between us. Each of us had said the hard things we needed to say while at the same time we had come to a place of understanding the other's point of view, even if we weren't comfortable with it. It was an enormous achievement on both our parts. I knew our complicated dance wasn't over, that it never would be, but we had certainly found a new rhythm.

I wanted to run and jump wildly, turn handsprings over the lawn. Instead I contented myself with sinking down to my knees on the carpet of fresh spring grass, reveling in its sweet scent, and calling out "Thank you, thank you" to whatever divine beings in the universe were watching over me—over us both!

*   *   *

Now that my relationship with my mother had made a big leap forward, I was ready to go on with my search. I called Yesterday's Children's yet again and this time heard a new message: "Our next meeting will be at seven on Monday evening, April 21st." That was only a week away. At last, I would have an opportunity to make contact with other adoptees.

When I arrived at the gathering that night, I was surprised and encouraged to see several other people there who were searching just like me. I also overheard a woman talking about the daughter she had given up as a baby.

"Not a single day goes by that I don't think about her, ache to know how she is, and hope to find her," she said with tears in her eyes.

I was spellbound. This was a lovely person, not some wayward woman of the streets like the old stereotypical picture of unwed mothers. Could my mother be just like her and wanting me to be part of her life?

Later I was put in touch with Diane, who had also been born in New York City and was looking for her mother. She told me that the identifying number on my original birth certificate was the very same as the one on my amended certificate. That was the one vital fact that was never changed (at least in New York City) when the amended document was created.

Diane said that I should go to the New York Public Library and ask to see the index of births for the year I was born. There, I could look through the names of all the people born in the city that year until I came to my number next to the date of my birth. Since my mother was unmarried, she would have given me her maiden name. By law, I couldn't have my father's last name unless he gave his consent—not a very likely possibility.

I could hardly wait to call the New York Public Library first thing the next morning, where I discovered such a book did indeed exist for the year 1934. I was even directed to a research assistant who could look up the information for me. When I discovered he wouldn't be available for three whole weeks, I was crushed. I was finally on the right path, and somehow I felt like the whole universe would be rooting for me.

Needing to talk to someone about my dilemma, I called Joan, the wife of Bill's brother Corson, in New Jersey. She had been supportive of my earlier attempts to get my birth certificate. Maybe she knew someone who could help me.

After I sputtered out what was happening, Joan said, "Listen, I'll find it for you. I have to go into New York sometime soon anyway."

I wasn't used to having people offer to do favors for me. All my life I had been the do-gooder who helped others. It felt strange and humbling to be on the receiving end.

Ten minutes later, Joan called back.

"I filled Corson in about your search. He's as excited as I am. Then we remembered we're going into New York tomorrow night for a concert. We can go to the library in the afternoon and look through the book. Just tell me that all-important number and your date of birth."

After I had given her the necessary information and thanked her profusely, I put down the phone and sat there in a daze. Maybe the universe was with me after all. Suddenly the prize that had seemed impossible to reach was hanging tantalizingly near. I had never expected the search to be this easy. If only I hadn't waited this long. What if I were too late? My birth mother might have died by now. How old would she be anyway? She was twenty-four when she had me. I had just turned forty-six, so she must be seventy. That wasn't too old, I reassured myself. She had to be all right.

I began to let my imagination run wild thinking about our first meeting. I would knock on her door. She would know I was coming and rush to open it. Staring at each other, we would be overwhelmed by the mirror image in front of us. No words would be necessary. We would just fall into each other's arms.

Reality hit as I was getting into bed that night when I remembered I had invited my adoptive mother over the next day to catch her up on my search. What would I do if Joan called in the middle of our conversation?

The following afternoon, I was making a valiant effort to concentrate on the newspaper when I heard my mother's car drive up. I had been praying I would hear from my sister-in-law before she arrived, but the phone had been silent all day. Trying to stay calm, I met my mother at the front door, ushered her into the den, and got her settled. Then I sat down opposite her and jumped right in.

"I wanted to catch you up with what has been happening in my search since the last time we talked," I began, trying to ignore the pounding of my heart.

"Oh, have you found out anything?" she asked guardedly.

Just then, the phone rang. *Oh, no, it can't be Joan, not right now.* I pounced on the receiver.

"Titia, are you sitting down? We found it!"

I almost dropped the phone. "Just a minute," I said quickly. "I have that information in the other room." I gave the phone to my mother, directing her to hang up when I got on the line in the kitchen. Reaching privacy, I picked up the receiver and said, "Thanks, Mom, you can hang up now."

I waited until I heard the line click.

"Oh, no," Joan gasped. "Your mother is there at this moment?"

"She is indeed. Unbelievable timing," I replied grimly. "But tell me what you found." My head felt as if it were about to explode.

"Well, the birth index for 1934 was pretty big. We just started at the beginning, looking down the columns of numbers, dates, and names. Corson took the left side of the page and I the right. My stomach went up into my throat every time I came to a May 9. Finally, after we had spent over two hours looking and were starting to feel discouraged, Corson grabbed my arm. He pointed to your number and then to the date, May 9, and finally to your name. Tears were falling down his cheeks; I began to cry as well. Listen, your name is Margaret MacGriffen."

There was silence as I tried to take in what Joan was saying.

"Titia, are you there? Do you understand? That's your name."

"I'm still here ... Margaret," I repeated, rolling the name around on my tongue. "What did you say the last name was again?"

"MacGriffen, M-A-C-G-R-I–F-F-E-N," she spelled out. "I ran as fast as I could to a public telephone to call you. We both felt terrible that we knew your name before you did."

"That's okay," I said lamely, but she was right. I had not realized until that very moment how much I wished that I had been the first person to see my given name.

After hanging up, I sat on the kitchen stool trying to take in the magnitude of this news.

I had just learned the name my birth mother had given me. I knew her last name too. I wanted to shout out loud, "My name is Margaret MacGriffen!" and cry with relief, but I didn't. Instead I pulled myself together, stuffed all my burgeoning feelings deep down inside my body, and made myself walk back into the den where my mother was waiting. I may have made some progress throughout the years, but it was pretty obvious that the role of being the good daughter was still hard for me to shake.

My mother regarded me suspiciously. "What was that all about? You look strange."

Forcing myself to smile, I said, "That was Bill's sister-in-law, Joan. She and Corson went to the New York Public Library this afternoon to look for my birth name."

To buy time, I tried to explain how they knew to do this. It came out all muddled. Finally I gave up and delivered the kicker, "She was calling to tell me they had just found my name in the index of births for 1934."

I could hardly look at her. Why did I still feel I was being disloyal?

"How amazing!" my mother said, her voice flat.

"Yes, isn't it? I never thought it would be so simple."

I waited a long time, expecting her to ask me what my name was. This was such a huge moment for me. Didn't she care about that? I was so focused in on myself that I couldn't believe she wasn't just a tiny bit interested in knowing this news as well. But why should she be? I had just unlocked the door to the past that she had counted on being shut forever since the day she brought me home.

"I know this must come as a shock to you. It is to me too." I was babbling, but I couldn't stand the silence. "I don't want you to worry. Even if I find my first mother, you will always be my real mother."

Her jaw relaxed slightly. "I'm certainly glad you think so."

She stood up, opened her black leather purse, and retrieved her car keys. "Amazing," she said again as I accompanied her to the front door, both of us teetering slightly.

She opened the door and was gone.

— 5 —

GREAT EXPECTATIONS

AFTER ALL THOSE MONTHS that had merged into years of inertia, incapable of taking charge of my life, I was excited to be following my heart's desire once again. In reality, I was too excited. Any thoughts of caution or discretion were quickly thrown out the window.

Two weeks later, I was walking up the massive stone steps of the New York Public Library on the way to see my name in the index of births. Bill and I met Corson and Joan at the front desk of the library, and the four of us headed down the long marble hallway to the genealogy department. There I found the 1934 black leather book in the stacks, brought it over to a table, and began going down the lists of numbers, birth dates, and names. My whole body began shaking when I came to my number, then the date May 9, and finally my name, Margaret MacGriffen.

Here was proof that I had existed before I was adopted, that I hadn't just dropped into this world like some traveler from outer space. I had a mother whose long line of family genes formed me. She had nurtured me in her womb, birthed and named me, and then had to give me away. I tried to imagine how I would feel if I had known I had to give up David, my firstborn, to never be allowed to see him or hold him to my breast. Just thinking about that made my heart ache. What did it do to my mother?

My sense of urgency escalated. I knew my mother's name, but

that wasn't my final goal. I never thought it would be. Now I had to find her. We rushed over to look for the name MacGriffen in the room where they kept the phone directories. One by one we combed through all the phone books for New England. When I opened the one for Connecticut, I struck pay dirt.

"Here it is," I announced excitedly. "There are two MacGriffens, a D. and a J. and they both live in Pellston."

Hurriedly, I wrote down the names and addresses because Joan reminded me it was time to leave for our dinner reservation before going to the theater. The idea of going to see a play seemed ludicrous to me. I was starring in my own drama right now, and the curtain was going up on the final act.

I had fantasized what it would be like when my mother and I finally met, but I had not given much thought to what I would say when I first made contact with her. Walking over to the restaurant, I talked with Joan about how to introduce myself. No question about it, I was way too driven to consider slowing down to think it through more carefully.

It would be years before I connected the compelling need to find my birth mother with the feelings of abandonment and loss I must have felt upon losing her the moment after I was born. But it was only too clear that I had wrestled with these two demons all my life. I see now that deep in my psyche, I held onto the fragile belief that if I could find my mother, she would heal me. What a tall order that was! And now this mother, maker of miracles, was only a phone call away.

Once we arrived at the restaurant, I went off and discovered a pay phone in a dark hallway on the way to the restrooms. Not a likely scene for reconnecting with the woman who had given me life, but nothing was going to stop me. Resolutely ignoring the bustling traffic around me, I dialed the first number.

A woman answered.

"Is this D. MacGriffen?" I asked trying to keep my voice steady while my heart pounded furiously.

"Yes, this is Darcy. Who is this?"

She sounded so young. She couldn't be my mother.

I told her she didn't know me but that my maiden name was MacGriffen. Oh, no, I hadn't meant to say that, but I guess I really had, otherwise it wouldn't have popped out. I said that I lived in Chicago but was here in New York with my husband researching my family history and that I was thrilled to find her name and only one other MacGriffen in the Connecticut phone book.

"I didn't know we had any relatives out in Chicago." Darcy sounded doubtful. "My dad will really be surprised to hear this."

Afraid that at any minute she might decide to hang up on this strange woman who had appeared out of nowhere claiming to be a relative, I quickly gave her the basic facts—that I was looking for a woman in her seventies or her two brothers, one a CPA and the other in life insurance.

"Would either of those be your father?"

"No, I'm afraid not. My dad is a civil engineer, and he's the youngest of three children."

"He's a civil engineer?" I repeated, feeling as if all the blood had just drained out of my body. This couldn't be the right one after all. But then in my mind's eye, I saw the sentence in the letter from Spence stating that when the man my mother loved had deserted her, she had turned to his best friend for support. That man was a civil engineer.

Whoops, I had to regroup here.

"Perhaps I've been looking for the wrong person. Maybe your father is the one I should talk to."

"He's not in town," she said quickly. "He's in Florida and has been ill for some time. He can't talk on the phone."

Please God, don't let him die before I see him, I prayed. Could he actually be my father? I hadn't ever considered searching for him. But I mustn't rush this (ignoring the obvious fact that rushing was just what I was doing, like in high speed). Better to talk with Darcy first since she seemed so forthcoming.

I asked about her life and discovered she owned a small gallery down on Long Island Sound. Impulsively, I inquired if she would be open to my husband and me dropping by tomorrow to see her since we were touring in the area. (Not that we had been planning to do that, but it seemed like a good idea all of a sudden.) I would probably have said no if I had been her, but Darcy was braver and more hospitable. She agreed and told me how to find her.

I walked back to our table in a zombie-like state.

"You won't believe this," I told the others, "but instead of my mother, I think I have found my father. I just talked to his daughter,

Darcy, who told me that her father was a civil engineer. The letter from the social worker at Spence stated my father was a civil engineer."

"We never even thought of that possibility," Joan said. "But this could work even better. He can tell you who your mother is. He'd probably be less threatened by your existence than she. Are you going to call him up now?"

"No, he's down in Florida and has been ill. Darcy sounded pretty protective of him, so I thought the best approach would be to see what we could learn from her. She said we could visit her at her gallery on the Sound tomorrow. Is that okay with you?" I asked, looking over at Bill. He gave me a thumbs-up.

"Everything is starting to move into high gear," I said, taking a large gulp of my wine. "I can't believe it's working out so easily."

We talked about the possibility of Darcy and her father welcoming me into their midst. He would tell me my mother's name, and I would find her too. Raising our glasses, we toasted the future and the success of my search.

I look back on that night and think how ingenuous we all were. I had reason to be more circumspect. My adoptive parents' fears and opposition to my search should have been a warning for me, but I wasn't thinking about any of that in my anticipation about meeting Darcy and, after that, the man I was sure was my father.

*   *   *

The next morning, Bill and I headed up the parkway out of New York in our rental car to meet my sister. Did I dare call her that? "My sister." I loved how it sounded on my tongue. Still stunned that I had found my father first, I felt pleased and hopeful that he had agreed to bestow his name on me. What a difference that would make in my search. The fact that his name was unusual and that there were only two MacGriffens in all the New England telephone directories was a stroke of luck as well.

Would Darcy and I look alike? Ever since I was old enough to understand fully what it meant to be adopted, I had always heard people comment on how much Wally looked like our mother. I wanted to look like her too, but of course I didn't. I moved from that hope to just wanting to find somebody out there who looked like me. It never happened until I produced David, my first blood relative. What a thrill it was when he turned out to resemble me, as did Frank a little and even Robin in later years. I still get a kick out of hearing people remark on that.

Darcy, on the other hand, was my connection to my past—that essential part of me I had never been allowed to know about. If we looked like each other, that would be better than any other kind of proof I could give her of our being related. It was the outward and visible sign of the family genes I had inherited.

We arrived at our destination and parked in front of Darcy's little gallery. Walking toward it, I clutched Bill's hand to keep myself grounded. But when Darcy opened the door, my heart sank. She was lovely, but there was not a shred of resemblance between us.

My big hope had just been shot down. We all introduced ourselves, admired the paintings and ceramics that she had created, and made small talk. Trying to be casual, I began asking Darcy about her family. I must have overdone it because Bill flashed me a warning glance. I made myself stop in mid-sentence.

With that, Darcy stepped into the gap and asked, not surprisingly, about me.

Here goes, I thought. *Don't blow it.* Taking a deep breath, I told her I was adopted as an infant from New York City, though my adoptive parents come from the Chicago area.

"They never wanted to talk about my past. I just knew that my birth parents had died soon after I was born. But ever since I have had my own children, I've wanted to know more about my roots."

"My father can tell you more about the clan than I can," she said quickly. "I'm going to call him tonight and tell him about you."

"Great, I'll call you tomorrow and find out what he has to say."

Mission accomplished.

When we were back in the car, I turned to Bill. "What do you think? Is she my sister? I was crushed when she didn't look like me at all."

"I don't know," he shook his head. "The key is to talk to her father. We don't know for sure if he is also your father, but you can bet he's never told her about you."

"You're right. I guess I'm not exactly a happy secret."

I sat pondering this thought. What if her father didn't want to acknowledge me because it would be too uncomfortable to explain my existence to his children or to his wife, for that matter, if he still had one? Darcy hadn't mentioned her in the conversation. Maybe he had never told anyone about this. Would he admit the truth to me now?

All my earlier exhilaration drained away. Should I really be doing this, coming into unsuspecting people's lives and announcing that I was a long-lost relative? And even worse, when I narrowed it down, to being a long-lost daughter? Would any of them want to know about me? I was beginning to grasp the impact that my appearance might have on the people in my birth family. It was altogether sobering.

*   *   *

Despite my belated doubts about the advisability of what I was doing, my first thought when I awoke the next morning was to call Darcy and find out what her father's reaction was to hearing about me.

She answered almost immediately and after a few brief words, announced, "I spoke to my father last night."

My nerve endings jumped into high alert. "What did he say?"

"He didn't have any idea what branch of the family you might be related to. He did remember that some distant cousins had gone west many years ago. He hasn't been in touch with any of them for a long time. But he says he wants to talk with you as soon as he comes back up here."

We exchanged addresses and phone numbers and hung up. I felt heartened. All I could think was, *He wants to see me. My father is interested in my existence.*

I decided to write to John MacGriffen and make my case. I didn't want to come right out and say he was my father, but I needed to let him know I had a number of facts that pointed toward him. I also wanted to reassure him that I was a responsible, mature person.

> *Dear Mr. MacGriffen,*
>
> *Now that you know of my existence and that I am searching for my family roots, I wanted to write you as soon as possible. First of all, I want to reassure you that I don't want to intrude into people's lives or cause anyone hurt. Darcy made it clear on the phone that*

from now on, I should deal directly with you and I agree with her.

Another reason I wanted to write is to let you know that I have had a very good and satisfying life. I was adopted by people who raised me well, and I married a wonderful man twenty-three years ago. We have three children who are now all in college. Yet despite my good fortune, it is immensely important to me to find out the truth about my origins.

You are the person who, I believe, can tell me what I want to know. I'd like to come and see you when you return to Connecticut this summer.

(I then explained how my search for my birth parents had led me to him.)

My strongest hope is that you will understand my need to come and have just one talk with you. After that, it will be up to you.

Sincerely,

Titia Ellis

I sent the letter off with a fervent prayer that John MacGriffen would receive it with an open heart. Five days later, while I was sitting at the kitchen table finishing up a paper for my research class, the phone rang. Preoccupied with what I was working on, I picked up the receiver and offhandedly said hello.

A deep, gravelly voice on the other end of the line announced, "This is John MacGriffen. I got your letter. How did you find out about the engineer part?"

I almost dropped the phone.

"I, uh, got that information from the Spence Adoption Agency," I replied in a shaky voice. "Would you like to see their letter?"

"I certainly would—later. But you can just read it to me now."

"Okay. It will take me a minute to find it."

"I can wait," he replied.

I put down the phone and ran outside to where Bill was weeding in the garden. "Oh, my God, it's John MacGriffen on the phone and he is mad. He wants to know how I knew about the engineer part. I'm getting the letter from Spence to read to him."

"I'll come in," Bill said quickly.

When I got back to the phone with letter in hand, I was breathless. "Here I am."

"Read it to me," he barked.

I made myself take a deep breath and began: "Your mother met your father through a mutual friend, a man whom she was in love with. When this friend suddenly married, she turned to your father for comfort. Your natural father was a college graduate who worked as a civil engineer and was interested in developing new products. He was described as tall with dark hair and eyes, and he had two brothers who were also college graduates."

When I finished, there was a long silence. The only sound was my heart beating like a huge drum inside my chest. Then he coughed and cleared his throat.

"There are a lot of inaccuracies in that letter. That part about the mutual friend that deserted her, though, that's true. Unfortunately, he was killed later in a car accident."

I sighed with relief. At least he admitted he was the man in the letter.

"It was indiscreet of you to talk so much to Darcy," he continued. "We are very close. She's extremely bright. When you told her that your birth parents had died shortly after you were born, she saw through that story. She told me that they always tell adopted children their natural parents have died."

"I'm sorry about that," I mumbled contritely.

"I have arterial fibrillation. I'm going up to Massachusetts General Hospital in June. And," he added in a harsh tone, "you have to accept the possibility that the birth certificate won't prove I am your father."

I couldn't think of anything to say to that.

"Do you realize that you have caused mental anguish to my family?"

"I didn't mean to," I replied. "I just believe I have the right to know where I come from like everyone else."

"I can understand that," he said softening a bit. "I lost my family at an early age too. My mother died when I was a year and a half. You need peace of mind."

I was relieved that he sounded more empathetic, but then he dropped a bomb. "Would you be willing to be searched by a matron for a listening device when we meet?"

I almost fell off my chair. "Do you really think I am that kind of person? This is not about blackmail. I just want to know the truth."

"How about your mother? Are you looking for her?"

"Yes, I am. I thought I had discovered her when I found my name recorded in the public library." I took a deep breath and thought, *Here goes.* "I've learned that in the case of a child born out of wedlock, New York law says the father's name cannot be used without his permission."

"I never gave permission to have my name used," he growled.

"Well, there it was," I said cautiously.

"We will talk about all this when we meet. You can call me next week. By then, I'll know when I am coming back."

"I appreciate your being willing to see me."

"Good-bye," he responded and hung up.

I put down the phone slowly. My hand was shaking.

"You're white as a sheet," Bill said. "What did he say?"

I repeated our conversation, ending with the part about him wanting me to be searched by a matron.

I cringed. "He must think I am an awful person."

"He's scared," Bill replied. "He doesn't know you. He'll change his mind when you meet and have a talk. Write him another letter and send a picture of yourself."

I liked his idea. Maybe seeing a photo of our whole family would give him a better feeling about me.

I sent off a letter and a picture to him the next day.

> *Dear Mr. MacGriffen,*
>
> *I've had so many thoughts and feelings whirling around inside me ever since your phone call. Listening to you helped me to understand you a little better and to see this whole difficult situation more from your point of view. The last thing I want to do is cause "mental anguish" for your family or in any way to hurt your relationship with Darcy. Looking back now, I too wish I had been more discreet. I hadn't planned to say*

my maiden name was MacGriffen, but I was so excited and nervous by the time I finally made contact with one of you that I just blurted that out. Apologies are pretty futile after the fact, but I am sorry about that nonetheless.

I hope you won't mind my saying that with a relationship as close as the one you and Darcy have (and I could tell how much each of you cared for the other by the way you both talked), the truth about me—which happened long before she was born—could never affect the love she has for you.

I am also concerned about your heart problems and though you were kind enough to reassure me that if anything happened to you, I wasn't to feel at fault, that's hard for me. Would it relieve some of your anxiety if I were to come down to see you in Florida within the next two weeks? That way you wouldn't have to spend a whole month anticipating and worrying about our time together.

I feel grateful that you understand how important it is for me to see you and learn the truth. If you will be willing to tell me what you can, I promise not to bother you or your family again.

And if it will relieve your mind even more, I will agree to be searched for a listening device before we talk. I just want you to know that as a result of your phone call, I feel a real caring for you and what you must be going through, as well as deep respect that you are willing to honor my request to meet with you.

I am enclosing a photo of my family that we sent out as a Christmas card two years ago.

Sincerely,

Titia

A week later as I was cleaning up the kitchen after lunch, the phone rang. When I answered, the familiar rough voice announced, "This is John MacGriffen."

My fingers clutched the receiver.

He started off tersely as before. "I'm leaving tomorrow. I want to get this done so my children won't be so upset."

"I feel terrible about your children," I responded, wondering what he'd thought of my letter but not daring to ask.

"Well, you'll make it right. And bring your husband along to help you evaluate what I have to say."

We arranged the date and time, he told me how to find his house, and then hung up.

I sat there, shaking all over. In one week's time, I would meet the man my mother said was my father. Despite the fact that he had been angry and abrupt on the phone, I had already formed an attachment to this crotchety character. It had begun when I listened to Darcy talk about their relationship. I envied the caring and love between them, much different from the coldness and silence between my father and me.

Oh yes, I was hoping for the moon from John MacGriffen. I wanted him to look like me. I wanted him to like me. I wanted him to acknowledge me as his daughter. But my longings didn't even end there. Most of all, I wanted him to tell me who my mother was. All this was to be accomplished in our first visit, which I had promised would be the last. I had forgotten the social worker's warning that no matter how much I was able to find out about my past, it would never be enough. I was willing to pledge anything in order to be granted the opportunity to meet my father. It was a promise I would not be able to keep.

Needing some fresh air after that phone call, I went out the back door and walked across the grass into the old apple orchard. Beyond in a clearing stood the ancient sycamore, its huge branches reaching up to the sky. I had always admired this tree, but today I felt drawn to stand directly in front of it. Reaching out, I rubbed my hands along its body. The bark had fallen off and the bare white trunk felt sensual beneath my touch, like solid velvet. Without thinking, I wrapped my arms around its circumference and rested my head against it. The strength and steadiness of the tree flowed through me, grounding me and bringing comfort. In that moment, something in me knew that by the time this search was over, I would never be the same again.

— 6 —

OUT OF THE SHADOWS

THE NEXT MORNING, MY mother phoned. "We haven't heard from you in a while," she began brightly. "I'm just calling to see how you both are."

Oh, dear. I could feel that all-too-familiar guilt snaking its way up through my body. I had been so obsessed by my dealings with Darcy and John MacGriffen that I hadn't given a thought to my adoptive parents for some time. Believe me, I had not wanted to. I was beginning to understand only too well why people who are adopted often choose not to stir things up by searching for their past, or at least electing to wait until after their adoptive parents have died.

As I slogged my way through this search dealing with my adoptive parents and now my possible birth father and his family, who were all experiencing such high voltage emotions of fear, shock, betrayal and anger, it was enough to make me question all over again whether it was worth it—no, whether I was worth it—when the result was such uproar in so many lives.

Beset by my own demons, I was sure my adoptive mother was threatened. Otherwise, she would never have made such an uncharacteristic call. But I had made that promise to keep her informed despite all my misgivings. Now the moment that I'd feared had come. Bracing myself, I told her there was more to report and made a date to come over the following morning.

My stalwart husband asked if I would like him to come along—

such a magnanimous offer. Oh my, was I ever blessed by some karma from a past life to have him along for this ride. Although I was tempted to accept his offer, I knew that wouldn't be right. These were my parents; this was my search and my very own drama that I had created. I was going to have to face it on my own.

When I walked into their home the next day, I found my parents already sitting in their comfortable chairs on each side of the fireplace in the living room reading the paper and drinking the last of their coffee; such a peaceful scene, and how I dreaded shattering it.

We started off with the usual discussion about the hot weather. Gearing myself up, I broke in before I completely lost my nerve.

"I want to tell you how I am coming in my search."

Dead silence fell over the room.

I made myself say, "There have been some new developments."

More silence.

"What's happening?" my mother finally asked.

How was I going to break this potentially upsetting news about my birth father? *Please be with me*, I prayed to whomever might be listening. Then I just dove in and told them the whole story.

"Mr. MacGriffen wants to see me, so Bill and I will be meeting with him next week," I concluded.

With that I sat back and tried to tell myself this would somehow all end up to be okay. How that would happen, I hadn't the slightest idea.

My parents were looking smaller and smaller. It was almost as if they were disappearing into their chairs. My mother reached in her pocket for her white handkerchief and began rolling it around in her hands. Her jaws were clenched. She looked over at me.

"This is all so quick."

"I know. I never expected it to happen this fast." I felt as if I had to apologize.

"Well," she said slowly, "it looks like you are determined to do this. We certainly can't stop you, no matter what we say or do."

Silence reigned while we digested these words.

"You're right," I replied. "I have to do this even though I don't like to see you in pain."

More silence. My mother studied her balled-up handkerchief with intense concentration. Her jaw was still working. "I am sure this man will be pleased to see the kind of person you've turned out to be," she said slowly.

"Thanks, Mom. That is a very generous thing to say."

I was surprised and touched by her response. My mother was not the type to offer compliments freely. Maybe there was room for hope after all. How I wanted that to be true, but this meeting was far from over.

I turned to my father who, as usual, had not uttered a word this whole time.

"How do you feel about this?" I asked, and then I looked at him more closely. Were those tears rolling down his cheeks?

"Why, Daddy, you're crying."

I regretted saying that the minute the words were out of my mouth, but I had never seen my father break down before in my whole life. Now I felt terrible.

He did not speak.

Rushing to reassure them, I said, "I want you both to know that I love you. If this man is indeed my birth father, it's not going to change my feelings toward you. I hope you can hear me."

My mother drew herself up. "I do believe you, Titia."

"I'm glad," I replied thankfully. "How about you, Daddy?"

He turned toward me for the first time. "I don't think you should do this. You should stop right now. If you are going to upset even one person, then that's wrong. How are Mr. MacGriffen's children going to feel about all this?"

I was taken aback by his reaction.

"Well," I said uneasily, "he seems to have a very close relationship with his daughter. I can't imagine something that happened long before she was born could hurt what they have now. My being conceived had nothing to do with Darcy or any of his other children or even his wife, seeing as he wasn't married back then."

I realized I was using just the same words to reason with him that I had written to John MacGriffen. They didn't sound all that convincing.

"No," my father said firmly, "it's still wrong. You will hurt them."

"I'm sorry you feel that way, but I don't agree with you. I think I have the right to know where I came from. John MacGriffen has to take responsibility for his part in that."

"I don't agree," he replied resolutely.

It was obvious that this discussion was heading toward nothing promising. I stood up.

"That's all I have to report for now. Thank you both for listening."

My mother stood as well. "I hope you get what you need from this man, Titia," she said.

"I really appreciate that, Mom," I said, giving her a big hug. I was deeply grateful for her support. Of course, I reminded myself, we were dealing with finding my birth father, not my birth mother. But still, she must realize that my birth father might tell me who my mother was. I looked over at my father, who was staring into the fireplace.

"Good-bye, Daddy."

No answer came from the inert figure. Was he going to be all right? I didn't have any strength left in me to find out. All I wanted was to retreat to the refuge of my home. I turned and walked out of the room.

Later when I had calmed down and thought about my father's unexpected response, I had to admit that part of what he had said was true—well, maybe everything. The MacGriffen family *was* upset by my abrupt entry into their lives. I could understand why, but I tried to persuade myself that I hadn't done something wrong. I was praying that once Mr. MacGriffen met me, he would see that I meant him no harm. I just wanted him to tell me the truth: that he was my father. Was that too much to ask for? Oh, yes, I had so much to learn back then.

But all that was down the road. Right now, I needed to talk with my adoptive father. Even though I was dismayed by his tears and strong words "Don't do this," his reaction caused me to consider what he was saying. Would it be possible for us to have a real conversation about all this? Giving us both a little time to recover from the encounter, I waited till the next morning to call and invite him over for tea.

"I can't do it today. I have an appointment," he replied irritably.

I could see this wasn't going to be easy. "How about the next day?"

"Oh, all right," he conceded, "but I still think you're wrong."

"We'll talk about that later."

When he arrived on the appointed day looking extremely dour, I ushered him into the den. My heart was beating rapidly. My father and

I had not been alone together, nor had any real conversation, since that luncheon in Chicago several years before when I had tried to persuade him to give me my original birth certificate.

I brought out iced tea in frosty glasses topped with fresh green mint from our garden. We started to talk awkwardly about the rain that had fallen that morning. I was so not looking forward to this, but finally I made myself begin.

"Daddy, I want to talk with you about my going to see John MacGriffen next week."

"Well, I've already told you what I think about your doing that," he declared. "I think it's dead wrong."

I was taken aback hearing my father speak his mind with such passion. It was a bit frightening and reminded me of when I was a child and he would get so angry at me. But then I told myself that I was a grown-up now, plus a family counselor, for heaven's sake, so why not draw on all that training right here in this moment.

I made an attempt at a smile and asked in my best therapeutic voice, "Why do you think it is wrong?"

He flashed back, "Because you will upset the MacGriffen family. That's why. You have no right to do that."

I was hooked immediately and blurted back that I was going to do it anyway, that I did have the right.

So much for trying to be a therapist with my own father!

He insisted I shouldn't do it—not if it would hurt anyone. We were at an impasse, hurtling our arrows back and forth with increasing force, when something in me woke up. Why was I doing this? I didn't want to fight with my father.

Out of my mouth came the words, "We have no connection with each other at all. I miss that."

Could I have really meant to say that—after all the times growing up that I'd interpreted his anger or his distance as a rejection of me?

My father looked surprised as well. Then he rose to the defense.

"What do you want me to do? Should I get down on my hands and knees on the floor and carry you around on my back like I did when you were little? I'm too old for that now."

What a sweet picture he had unintentionally painted. I wished I could remember him carrying me around like that.

"You're right, it's too late for that. I am just asking to have an adult relationship with you. We don't even know each other. I want to be able to tell you about my work," I continued, "and all sorts of other things."

What these other things would be I had no notion, but somehow I had a feeling that my father and I could find lots of things to talk about.

My father must have been in shock at this one-eighty turn of events. He sat there not saying a word.

But I didn't seem to be done yet.

"I don't know anything about you either, and that makes me sad."

Was this really happening? Was I trying to pull the man in the shadows out into the light? It had always been my mother who had been the prime focus of my attention.

My father was silent for a long time, staring down at the carpet. *Oh please, don't let him ignore what I had just said.*

Then he spoke, his voice low and shaky.

"Do you know it's very lonely for me since my eyes started going? I can hardly read the paper anymore. My friends are all gone. And, of course, your mother is always working on her book." His voice trailed off.

My heart leapt toward him.

"Daddy," I said gently, "I had no idea you were feeling that way. It must be awful to be losing your sight. And I know how much time Mom is spending on her book these days."

"Yes, well," he began, sounding embarrassed. He studied his watch. There was a long silence. "I have to go home." His voice became firmer. "It's six o'clock. Your mother will be waiting for me so we can have a cocktail and watch the evening news."

With that, he started to pull himself up from his chair.

"Don't go yet, please," I begged, but he shook his head.

Before I could say another word, he had walked out of the room. I heard the front door open and then shut while I just sat there on the couch and let myself feel rejected all over again. But then a voice inside me said, *Wait a minute, something has changed.* I am different and look at what my father just admitted to me. He was really vulnerable. Maybe, just maybe, this could be the beginning of a new way of being with each other.

Looking back on this time, I see that my adoptive parents did indeed feel betrayed by my wanting to look for the people who had conceived and birthed me. These people who had adopted me felt they had become my true parents. They had given me their name, loved and nurtured me to the best of their ability. Never in their wildest imagination did they think I would turn around and say I wanted to find my "real parents" (which was how they heard that). No wonder they could only conclude that I didn't love or appreciate them, despite all they had done on my behalf.

Fortunately my mother and I had been having a conversation, difficult as it was, about all this for a long time. I believe this helped her move beyond her pain, to see that my search had nothing to do with her, and to trust me when I said how much I loved her.

But my father and I had spoken only once about my search back when I was at the beginning. Perhaps his strong objection to my searching came from his feeling a deep hurt and lack of appreciation. I could understand that. But I was pleased that he now felt safe enough with me to be able to talk about the anguish of going blind and that my mother was spending more time writing her book than with him. This was a big step forward for him and for us.

And I suppose I had better admit at this juncture that just maybe my father's missing my mother's company might bear a slight resemblance to how my own long-suffering husband must have felt as I spent years searching for my birth parents and then countless more years writing about it. What wonderful irony. For the first time, I was seeing that although I was not related by blood and didn't resemble her, I was still more like my adoptive mother than I had ever imagined.

— 7 —

ARE YOU THE ONE?

THE DAY ARRIVED WHEN we were to meet with John MacGriffen. Alternating between wild excitement and total panic, I knew that the success or failure of my search depended on this encounter. And let's face it—my two phone contacts with this potential candidate for the starring role of my father had hardly filled me with confidence. Foreboding might be a more apt description. How was I going to break through his tough New England exterior, which most likely was a cover-up for his own fear? All I could do was speak from my heart.

Driving over to his house, I glanced at Bill, who was strangely silent. "What's going on?" I asked, needing to make contact before we walked into the lion's den.

"I'm just wondering," he said bleakly, "what it's going to be like if this visit doesn't meet your expectations."

I flinched. That wasn't what I wanted to hear. To bolster my sagging spirits, I replied forcefully, "Well, I still believe that John MacGriffen is my father, despite his denial. Why would he have been that upset on the phone otherwise? I just have to pray he will tell me the truth about himself and my mother too. He's the only one who knows her last name. Without that, I'll never find her."

Bill's only response was to shake his head and stare with resignation at the road before us.

When we arrived promptly at ten, John MacGriffen was just driving his car into the garage. He came out, a somber expression on his face, and walked in measured steps toward us. My stomach was in spasms. He was a tall man with gray, dark hair coming to a widow's peak on his forehead, dark brown eyes, and an aquiline nose.

Once again, there was not the slightest hint of resemblance between us. Was I finally going to have to let that dream die, or could it be possible I looked like my mother instead? After awkward introductions and shaking of hands, we followed him into the house. Pointing to the beige couch facing the fireplace he said, "Please sit down. Can I get you some coffee?"

While he was in the kitchen, I looked over at Bill, rolling my eyes. "We sure don't look alike, do we?" I whispered.

"No," he whispered back, "but I like him so far."

"Me too."

Mr. MacGriffen returned with three mugs, placed them on the weathered wooden coffee table in front of us, and settled himself on the other side in a large brown leather chair. For the next twenty minutes, we made small talk. Well, not we—he and Bill did. They chatted about how he had lived here thirty-seven years, his collection of antique clocks, and the colleges they had attended. Not one of his remarks was addressed to me. What's more, he didn't even look in my direction when I tried to interject myself into the conversation. It was as if I didn't exist.

But, of course, that was the whole point. John MacGriffen didn't want me to exist, right from day one. Now, forty-six years later, here I was back in his life, dragging a sack filled with expectations and needs. My very presence in this room said it all—I'm here, I'm your daughter, tell me you want me in your life. And he was having nothing to do with me.

By now, I had had enough of being ignored. I was prepared to stand up, shout, and do something wild and outrageous to make him notice me.

As if he had read my mind, John MacGriffen paused in mid-sentence, turned, and spoke directly to me. "I want to tell you my story."

He had my instant attention.

"My family was from Scotland," he began. "They lived on the Isle of Skye, where they earned their living as sheep herders and weavers."

I was totally on board. This was what I needed to hear.

"My father's family married into the MacGregor clan. They were kicked out of Scotland in the late 1800s during the clearings and settled in Nova Scotia. Life was very hard there. Eventually my parents moved to Boston. My mother died when I was a year and a half."

He recited all this in a monotone while I listened raptly, not wanting to miss one word. It even passed through my mind fleetingly that I would have liked to tape our interview, the way I recorded all the people I interviewed for my dissertation. Wouldn't that have gone over well!

He paused for a sip of coffee and looked over at us. "Is this interesting to you?"

"Oh, yes," I responded eagerly. "Please continue." Would he be telling us all this if it weren't my history too?

He told about his schooling, how he got a scholarship to MIT. His best friend there was a medical student who had one girlfriend in New Hampshire and one in Boston.

Here he paused and looked straight at me. "That woman in Boston was your mother."

My heart jumped into my throat; my whole body felt weak. He was admitting he knew my mother. That must mean he was my father. Now I was going to learn what really happened to her.

Mr. MacGriffen continued. "She lived nearby in a boarding house for girls which was very strict. They couldn't go out with men unchaperoned. And they were only allowed to talk to the men who came to see them while sitting in little booths that had curtains around them. Some old lady was always running around pulling up the curtains to check on them."

I tried to imagine my mother entertaining a man in this manner. It seemed absurd. How on earth could she have gotten pregnant if she were being watched that closely?

"I met your mother when my friend fixed me up with a blind date. It wasn't with her, though," he added hastily. "I actually only saw her two times. Finally his girlfriend in New Hampshire came down and demanded that they get married. I was the best man at their wedding.

"Several months after that, with no advance warning, two men came up from New York to see me." His voice became louder and indignant.

"They said that the girlfriend from Boston was pregnant by me. She had moved to New York to be with her brothers and needed help to pay for the baby. Her brother was one of the men; the other was a lawyer. I was shocked." A pained look crossed his face. "I remembered that I had seen her walking along the road one night in the rain and offered her a ride, but she refused. I guess she was pregnant by then and didn't want me to see. Later, I had to go down to New York, where she and I had a very difficult meeting. Your mother became hysterical."

He looked accusingly at me. He was still angry; it was as if it had all happened yesterday. "I had to pay that lawyer $200 when she gave up the child for adoption."

My mind was racing. He's talking about my mother and me; he came down to see us. And he's admitting that he paid the lawyer. It must mean that he's the one. Oh, I was looking so hard for proof.

"Did you ever see her again?" I blurted out.

He shook his head vehemently. "No, I never did. I have no idea what happened to her."

"Anyway," he resumed in a calmer manner, "my friend went on to become a great anesthesiologist who developed some new technique. Much later, I confronted him about being the father of his former girlfriend's child. He totally denied it. I thought maybe there was a third party."

He leaned back in his chair. "That's really all I can tell you."

I sat there overwhelmed. He was trying to convince me that he wasn't the one, but I didn't buy it. If he really wasn't my father, why didn't he confront his friend as soon as my mother's brother and the lawyer came to see him?

Now my heart needed to speak. "I feel confused and disappointed by your story. Can you tell me anything more about my mother?"

"I don't know much. She was short and dark-haired and came from some place in Vermont."

"Do you know where in Vermont?"

"No idea. I just remember she was a secretary."

"Can you tell me her name?" I asked, trying to keep the desperation out of my voice.

"You mean you don't know your mother's name?" He looked

flabbergasted. "Well, I'm certainly not going to tell you that. She is a little old lady of seventy by now, probably a grandmother with a whole big family. You would disrupt her life terribly if you got in touch with her, if you moved in boisterously."

I bristled at that. "I wouldn't move in 'boisterously,' as you put it. And just maybe she would be happy to see me, to know that I am alive and well and have had a good life."

"No," he said positively, "I don't think it's a good idea."

We were at a standstill. My mind was spinning. *How can I possibly get through to him?* I decided to try another tack. "Why is your family upset?"

"Well, they are worried about me and my bad heart. Everybody told Darcy she had been too open with you. I hope you will decide to write her and reassure her that I am not your father after our talk. Your story to Darcy—anyone with any intelligence could see through that. I didn't know what kind of person you were, whether you wanted vengeance."

"Vengeance is the last thing on my mind. As I wrote in my two letters to you, all I want is the truth."

"I'm telling you that," he said testily.

"Will you tell me the name of the mutual friend, now that he and his wife are dead?"

"No, I can't do that. There are three girls, all grown, with families who could be hurt. Besides, he said he wasn't your father." He folded his hands impassively in front of him. "We will never know the truth."

I looked over at Bill. Maybe Mr. MacGriffen would listen to him.

Picking up on my unspoken plea, my husband jumped into the fray.

"I think it's important that you tell Titia her mother's name."

"No. It would have a terrible effect on your mother to find out about you after all these years," he replied stonily. It sounded as if he were speaking about his own reaction.

I decided to play my trump card once again. "The State of New York says that an illegitimate child cannot have its father's name unless the father gives his permission."

"I told you I never gave my permission," he thundered.

"Was my mother's first name Margaret?"

"No."

"Well, what was her name?" Bill asked.

Magically, as if the correct code had been entered, Mr. MacGriffen relented. "It was Dorie."

"Is that short for Dorothy?" I asked.

"I don't know."

"Can you at least tell us what nationality she was?" I didn't like being forced to play this cat-and-mouse game with him, but what were my choices?

"I have no idea."

I leaned back against the couch, fighting to keep tears from welling up in my eyes. Just knowing her nickname would never be enough to find my mother. Where had I ever gotten the idea that I could win this man over?

"I knew you would be disappointed when you heard my story," he said, looking at me in a friendlier way. "That's why I wanted your husband here. I had thought of telling it to Bill first to see if he thought you could handle it."

"I would never have agreed to that," I declared, pulling myself together. Who did he think I was, some fool woman who couldn't control herself? But since he had said my mother got hysterical at their meeting, he would expect me to do the same. Why wouldn't she be upset? She had just had a baby and had to give her up. Then she had to deal with this irate man who didn't want to admit he was the father.

"What do your parents feel about this search of yours?" he asked to my surprise.

"They have been threatened," I admitted, "but my mother has come around. She said she hoped I would get what I needed from you. My father is still angry. I feel envious of your relationship with Darcy. I have never been close to my father."

He glanced at his watch.

No, I thought, *we can't leave it like this.* I had to try one more time.

Looking him squarely in the eye, I asked, "Mr. MacGriffen, will you tell me on your honor as a gentleman whether or not you are my father?"

"I am not your father, and if I were, I wouldn't have given you up," he stated forcefully.

I had half expected him to deny being my father, but I was totally taken aback by his saying that if he had been, he wouldn't have given me up. For some reason, it made me feel good to hear that. Looking back on that statement, it makes no sense at all. He was a poor student struggling to make ends meet. The idea of him raising an illegitimate child by himself was crazy.

"I don't think my mother had many options," I told him, feeling protective of her. "It would have been pretty hard for anyone to raise an illegitimate child in the 1930s."

"Oh, plenty of people managed it back then. This kind of thing has been going on a long time," he responded almost cavalierly.

I wanted to disagree with him, but I controlled myself. I needed to try one more time to get her name. "Could you think some more about telling me my mother's last name? It means everything to me."

"I am thinking," he said curtly. "It's a very difficult position to be in."

With that he stood up. We were being dismissed. He shook my hand and said, "Good-bye, Titia."

It was the first time all morning that he had called me by my name. At least I felt acknowledged by him.

"I will write Darcy," I promised, eager to do anything that might win him over.

"It's not a big thing," he replied casually. "She's not that worried."

Well, you must be, I thought, *to ask me to do that.* Again it made me suspicious that this man wasn't telling me the truth. But I had confronted him enough. He held the key to finding my mother. So I just said, "Thank you for agreeing to meet with us. I appreciate it."

"I know you will do the right thing," he replied.

We said good-bye. John MacGriffen opened the door for us and then stood in the driveway, his arms folded, watching as we got into our car and drove off.

I sat rigid in my seat, staring straight ahead. All I could focus on was Mr. MacGriffen saying, "I'm not your father."

Bill leaned over and touched my hand. "Would it help to talk about it?"

"What's there to say?" I asked dully. "He said he wasn't my father. There's nothing more I can do."

"Do you believe him?"

"I don't want to, but he was pretty convincing."

"When he said if he had been your father he wouldn't have given you up, that got to me." Bill admitted. "He seemed like an honorable man who was telling the truth."

"I felt the same way," I agreed. "It hurts worse because by then I admired him and really wanted him to be my father."

"Still, there are many unanswered questions. It doesn't add up," Bill conceded.

"Then he refuses to tell me the name of that man who he was hinting all along was my real father."

For a while, I was lost in reflection. "What does it matter anyway? That guy is dead. But the worst part is that he won't give me my mother's name. It's just too cruel. I have a right to know that, and he's the only one who can give it to me."

"He did say he was thinking about whether to tell you your mother's name," Bill reminded me.

"I remember, but I can't imagine that he will. He's so angry at me."

My dream of finding my birth parents had crashed down around me. I had nothing more to say.

*   *   *

When we arrived back home, my first act was to keep my promise to Mr. MacGriffen to write Darcy. In my letter I told her we had had a good visit with her father but regretted that there seemed no way I was related to her branch of the family. I said that I was disappointed, as they both seemed like such good people.

I sent that letter off with a heavy heart. Even though I still clung to the belief that I was his long-lost daughter, I had just given up my claim to any blood connection to John MacGriffen and his clan. Writing it should have been the final act of my search, but I couldn't let go. I clung to the hope that since I had done what he asked of me, he would be pleased and relieved. Maybe now he would relent and tell me my mother's last name.

But I wasn't going to sit there in limbo waiting for him to call, either. First, I persuaded our family doctor to write the New York Infirmary, listed on my amended birth certificate as the place of my birth, and ask for legal proof of my arrival into this world. The hospital wrote back that all their records before 1950 had been destroyed in a fire. One down—try another tack.

I sent a letter to the Bureau of Vital Statistics requesting my original birth certificate. Back came a curt note saying I was forbidden by law to have access to my birth certificate. Another one down.

I persisted, this time asking a friend who was a travel agent to write saying that I, her client, needed my original birth certificate to obtain a passport for travel abroad. It did absolutely no good at all. Once again the powers that be refused our request.

✳   ✳   ✳

A few weeks later, Bill and I flew east to attend the wedding of Joan and Corson's daughter. The ceremony was taking place in the Chapel at Middlebury College in Vermont, my birth mother's home state. The pain of being that close to my mother with not a clue but the nickname, Dorie, as a way to find her was hard to bear.

Years after this, I would learn that Vermont is a center for dowsers— people who go around holding divining rods that point down to the earth if there is water below the ground. Later they expanded out into searching for lost objects and missing persons, often with great success. Could one of those dowsers have found Dorie for me? I certainly would have tried that avenue had I known it existed.

On the other hand, I was excited to be attending this family gathering, especially since all our children were to be present. After the rehearsal dinner on Friday night, everyone ended up back at the Middlebury Inn, singing all the old songs from summers spent together at our camp up in Canada. It was a magical evening. Leaning back against my husband's shoulder, listening to his beautiful tenor voice blend with our children's as they sang "Green Pastures," I was filled with joy. Later I noticed Robin had slipped out of the room to call her boyfriend, Mark, who was house-sitting for Bill and me. Soon she hurried back into the bar and grabbed my hand.

"Mom, come quick. Mark says there's a handwritten letter for you from Pellston, Connecticut. Maybe it's from that man you thought was your father."

My heart leapt. Could Mr. MacGriffen have changed his mind?

Was he going to admit that he was my father or, at least, give me my mother's name?

I picked up the phone, my heart pounding. "Hi, Mark. Can you open the letter and read it to me?"

"Sure," he replied. "There's a black-and-white photo of a man and a short note, which says: 'Here is the man your mother was in love with. His name is Keith James and he was from Truro, Massachusetts. The enclosed picture was taken at his wedding and I should like to have it back. But even though all the evidence points to his being the one, I would caution you not to assume he is your father.' That's all—no signature or anything."

As much as I had prayed that John MacGriffen would not cut me out of his life, I was still surprised to hear from him. That he had given me the name and photo of the other man in question was a hopeful sign.

Once again, I asked the question: Would I look like Keith? Will there be that shock of recognition when I get home and see his face?

At the same time, as grateful as I felt toward Mr. MacGriffen, I still wanted my mother's name most of all. We were locked in a contest of wills, but he was the dealer who held all the winning cards.

The day after the wedding, Bill and I strolled around the town of Middlebury. In a local crafts store, we came upon a beautiful handmade quilt, with a white background decorated with graceful green circles. The shopkeeper told us it was a wedding ring pattern.

"I love this," I told Bill. "Let's get it for our bed as a remembrance of Vermont and my mother. Who knows if we will ever be back in this state?"

Flying back on the plane, I thought about how glad I was to have been at that wedding. Yes, my birth mother, undiscovered and unknown, was often on my mind, but I realized that even if I never found her, I already had a family. And it was a wonderful one. I came perilously close to giving all this up when Bill and I were on the verge of divorce. Thank God, I, no we, had made the right choice.

When I returned home, I immediately picked up the photo of Keith James. My heart sank. He was blond with a square head and jaw. Though his eyes were dark like mine, we didn't look at all alike. I had the photo blown up as large as possible to see if there were any hidden similarities, but none were apparent. Another strikeout.

Before I relate what I did next, I must preface it with a most relevant piece of information. I am born under the sign of Taurus and, for those who are not into astrological signs, the distinguishing trait of us Tauruses is our stubbornness or stick-to-it-ness until we manifest what we want. I hope this makes it self-evident why I just couldn't stop bothering poor unsuspecting John MacGriffen. I had no say in the matter. The stars had preordained it.

I sent the original picture back with a note thanking him for his kindness in supplying it and the name of the other man. And then I implored him one more time to send me my mother's name, ending with the words:

"You are my only hope."

— 8 —

A LARGER PLAN

SOME INNER WISDOM FINALLY kicked in, advising me to turn my energy toward my adoptive parents and stop waiting for answers from John MacGriffen. Here were the people, right in my own backyard—literally—who raised me, loved me, and were standing by me even now.

When I told my adoptive mother that Mr. MacGriffen had rejected me as his daughter, I was touched when she said, "I'm sorry it didn't work out for you."

My heart was opening up to her. I had stood up to her and claimed my right to search for my birth parents. Scared she would lose my love, she had resisted my efforts in every way she could. But that period seemed to be behind us now. Could it be possible we might find some new way of being with each other that was more fulfilling than what we had had in the past?

Could that even happen someday with my adoptive father? I was just beginning to step out of my old thought patterns and behaviors to see that my own soul and the universe itself might have a much larger plan awaiting me than I had ever imagined.

The timing seemed propitious. My parents were planning a party to celebrate their fiftieth wedding anniversary that was coming up in three months at which, according to family tradition, I would be expected to make a toast. Having put them through so much anguish with my search, I wanted to give them the ultimate gift by honoring them as my parents in front of all their friends.

But first, my father was celebrating his eightieth birthday, and I offered to host his party at our house. This was breaking the long-standing pattern of my parents always celebrating their birthdays with a party in their own home. I was pleased when they accepted my invitation. On a warm summer's night in June, twelve of us, family and friends, sat down to a festive meal that I had prepared and my children served.

After my father had blown out all the candles on his cake, Robin stood up and gave a beautiful toast to her grandfather, thanking him for who he was and for all he meant to her. He was deeply moved, as were all the rest of us.

I realized I should toast him as well, but I was so busy with the dinner that I hadn't thought about preparing something to say. Launching in, I felt awkward, unable to come up with any loving words in contrast to what my daughter had freely spoken. When I finished, my father turned away, disappointed. I felt the same.

*   *   *

I broke another tradition a week after that party by deciding at the last moment to ask my parents to visit us up in Canada. There had always been an unspoken agreement between Bill and me that our vacation time in Canada was reserved just for our family. Since we lived next door to my parents, we saw them often enough as it was. But the greater reason was my father's and my relationship. I hadn't wanted to have to deal with him any more than was necessary, and certainly not while I was up at our sacred retreat.

Since he had opened up with me about his pain, however, I wanted to see if we could build on that conversation. Maybe I could get closer to my mother as well. I wasn't sure if they would even want to come, for that matter, as we were offering a pretty late invitation and they had heard how rustic our place up there was—with no electricity, phones, or TV.

But, surprise! My parents accepted our invitation with alacrity. When they arrived, we had a full schedule planned for their entertainment. The first afternoon, after picnicking out on the deck and cruising around in our boat, I turned to my mother and said, "You're looking wonderful. I can't remember having seen you wear anything except dresses and stockings all these years, but those slacks look great on you. And I like your hair ruffled by the wind. It's very becoming."

"I'm not sure my hairdresser would agree," she laughed, but I could see she was enjoying this new freedom.

As for my father, at every opportunity I made an effort to bring him into the conversation by asking his opinion on whatever topic we touched on. Before long, he was chiming in without my prompting. What's more, he had a lot of interesting ideas to offer.

Another side of my father emerged the next morning as he watched Bill and me dive off the dock into the chilly water below.

"I'd like to go swimming too," he ventured. "Are there some steps I could walk down? Don't think I'm up to diving," he laughed.

I tried to dissuade him. The stairs leading into the water had been blown away during the winter.

My father was undeterred. "What about rigging up a rope that I can slide down?"

With a questioning glance back at me, Bill said, "We can try."

The two of them went off looking for a suitable place. Soon there was a shout from Bill. "Go look at Pops!"

My mother and I rushed around to the other side of the cabin. There was my father holding on to a rope that had been tied to a pine tree. He was attempting to slide off a huge, flat rock into the channel.

My mother grabbed my hand, "Is that safe?"

"As long as he keeps his footing and holds onto the rope, I guess it is," I answered, holding on to her hand tightly, as I wondered if my eighty year old father had the strength to do that. His body looked so white and vulnerable in his blue swimming trunks. When he reached the water, he totally disappeared beneath it for an instant. We all gasped, but then his head bobbed up. Waving to us, he splashed around for several minutes in the choppy water. When he got out, still holding onto the rope, and clambered across the rocks looking like an ancient seal, everyone cheered.

"Great job, Daddy," I said as he was toweling himself off. "You looked like you were having fun out there."

"It's perfect water," he declared, breathing hard. "I plan to do that every day I'm here."

I was witnessing a side of my father I had never seen before. He was courageous and determined to prove himself, despite his aging body.

We spent their last evening sitting out on the deck watching the sun make a stunning farewell, shooting orange, pink, and purple beams across the sky, which were reflected in the water below.

"Wow, this is beautiful, kiddo," my father said, using the old term of endearment he had called me when I was young.

I found I liked being called that. It brought back a memory from my childhood with him that was good. More than that, I was happy that he was showing an easy affection toward me. We had come a long way from all the years of strained silence between us, not to mention the tension created by his strong opposition to my contacting John MacGriffen.

"Yes," echoed my mother, "we've had such a good time in your beautiful place. It's been a treat to share it with you."

I couldn't help thinking how gracious they were, never making a dig about how long it had taken me to invite them. Nor had they made any mention about the lack of amenities that they were used to back home. I felt grateful we had asked them. And I realized it never would have happened had I not embarked upon this formidable search, which was providing one most unexpected outcome—that of bringing me into a closer relationship with my adoptive parents than I had ever thought possible.

"You've been such good sports," I said. "I'm glad you came."

The day after they flew home, my father contracted pneumonia and had to be put in the hospital. I was sure it came about from his daring swimming escapades off our rocks. What a relief when he was well enough to be released. It made me see how much I was looking forward to getting to know this man whom I had spent a big part of my life trying to avoid.

*   *   *

When we returned home two weeks later, I invited my mother to have lunch uptown at one of my favorite restaurants. That might not sound like a big deal to many people, but I couldn't remember when we had last eaten out alone together. Thinking this would be a good time to plumb her memory, I asked what she thought was the major ingredient that made her marriage of fifty years a success. A little bit of self-interest came in here because I have to admit that by now the pressure to say something that would be a fitting tribute to my parents at their big celebration was beginning to weigh heavily on me.

My mother put down her fork and thought for a minute.

"I think the reason we have done so well," she said, "is because your father never stopped me from doing anything I wanted. He always encouraged me."

"That's quite a gift."

She continued, "Yes, your father really respected me, just as my father did."

"How did you know that your father respected you?" I got diverted here. I knew my mother had always adored her father, and I wanted to know more about her childhood.

"My father was a wonderful man." She was silent for a moment. "He was the one who was always kind and understanding every time the doctors said I had to have another operation."

"Tell me more about the operations. I've never really known what was wrong."

"Oh, my goodness." My mother cast a furtive glance around the room as if assessing how safe it was to continue. "I had all these dire female problems."

I was shocked. "How awful for you."

"Yes, it was terrible. The doctors told me when I was ten years old that I would have to undergo surgery to correct it all. And after that first one, there were more operations. Every time I was told I had to have another one, I would burst into tears. My mother would spank me for being such a baby."

"How could she do such a thing? That's inhuman."

"Well, you knew my mother. She was pretty tough. But my father would bring me into his study, take me up on his lap, and hold me while I cried. He would try to explain why it was important that I have these operations. If I didn't, he said, I couldn't have babies when I grew up and got married. I'd tell him I didn't want to get married, and I certainly didn't want to have any babies. He'd smile, pat my back, and say that someday I would change my mind and be glad I went through all this."

I sat there at a loss for words. I had never in my life had such a personal conversation with my mother. Reaching over, I took her hand and began stroking her delicate fingers. "I don't know how you survived it."

My mother wasn't finished. It was as if a logjam had broken loose. "When your father and I went off on our honeymoon, we visited a world-famous specialist in Germany about my problems. He stated that it was very unlikely I would ever be able to have children."

"What a thing to hear after all those years you'd suffered."

"Yes, it was a devastating blow, but soon after your father and I came home, we wrote to Spence asking to adopt a baby. Your sister, Leslie, came the following year and then we got you a year and a half later."

"And in the end," I added, "you proved them all wrong by producing Wally, the miracle child."

"Yes I did," she nodded happily.

"I'm honored that you would tell me all this. It makes me feel very close to you."

It was true. I was filled with tenderness for my mother upon learning all she'd endured. At the same time I was appalled that her own mother had treated her so cruelly. Considering everything she had been through, she had done a pretty good job raising us. No wonder it was hard for her to show much physical affection, but she had managed the best she could.

I thought back to times she had been there for me with sage advice on how to handle problems with friends at school or when she presented me with a notebook containing all the letters I had written home from my college junior year abroad that she'd saved and had typed up. And there were the innumerable visits she had made to the hospital to cheer me up throughout my back operations. I realized why she understood what I was feeling, after all the difficult surgeries she had to go through.

By now, we were the only ones left in the restaurant. When I asked for the bill, my mother brought out her wallet to pay. "No," I demurred, "this is on me."

Stepping out into the hot sunlight, I was still in awe that I'd had such an intimate conversation with my mother and in such a public place.

"You're a pretty special woman," I told her.

"Well, you're pretty good yourself," she replied.

We both laughed as we walked with our arms around each other back to my car.

— 9 —

SPEAKING MY TRUTH

THROUGHOUT THE YEARS, MY parents had delighted in throwing parties to commemorate important events in their lives. There had been a graduation dance for my mother when she attained her BA degree at the age of fifty-eight and large dinner parties commemorating their thirtieth and fortieth anniversaries. At their fortieth, believe it or not, my women's singing group was the featured entertainment. I like to think we had upgraded our act by then, but we still had a lot of fun. Now the big day—their fiftieth wedding anniversary—had finally arrived. The celebration that night was to be their pièce de résistance. And I was not looking forward to it.

Although I had been working on my toast to honor my parents for several weeks, I was unable to come up with just the right words to show how much I loved and admired these people who were still hurt by my need to find my original parents. First, I tried listing all their numerous accomplishments, but that felt overwhelming. After many false starts, I decided to be more personal, to talk about them from my view as their daughter, but I got mired down in the places where I had felt unloved by them instead. That was definitely not the way to go. I gave up and waited for inspiration to flow through me in some miraculous fashion. To my dismay, it never showed up.

To say that I was feeling just a touch of panic because I had nothing prepared to say would be an understatement. Stopping over at my parent's home that morning, I went out and peeked inside the tent

84

that had been erected on the west lawn. The scene was chaos. People were rushing about, setting up tables and chairs, unpacking cases of wine and champagne, and putting white and pink roses and green ivy into large vases. Inside the house, I found my mother upstairs in her study. She and Margaret Wells, her faithful secretary of twenty years, were bending over a card table making final adjustments to the seating plan for dinner.

"You're looking very relaxed on this busy day," I observed admiringly. "How many people are coming?"

"Ninety-eight and only three have dropped out," she replied, as she deftly moved one of the place cards to another table on the diagram. "Now I have to go talk to the caterers. I'll see you later at the party."

That afternoon, I gathered my family together out on our terrace. I was grateful that all our children had made it home from college for this occasion, and I had a favor to ask of them.

"I need your help. I've not been able to come up with anything to say to my parents tonight. Do you think we could figure out some kind of skit or song that we could perform together as a family?"

No one would heed my plea. They all had written their own speeches. David, our musician, had even composed a song that he was going to perform with his guitar.

I turned to my husband. "Surely you'll help me? You know how hard I've tried to write something."

"I know this is difficult for you," Bill replied, "but I honestly think you need to give your own toast. Why don't you talk about what good sports they were up in Canada this summer?"

"Don't worry, Mom," said Frank, wanting to encourage me, "You'll be fine."

While I was getting dressed that evening, I decided that Bill's suggestion of talking about all of us up in Canada wasn't worthy of the occasion. The pressure I put upon myself to come up with the perfect acknowledgement felt like more than I could bear. Yet as much as I wanted my family to carry me, I had to admit that they were right to refuse me. This talk had to be done on my own or not at all. Would that last option be what I would be forced to choose ?

We arrived at the party and were greeted by my parents, glowing with hospitality and happiness at the entrance to the tent. My mother's long, pink satin gown highlighted her slim figure. To my eyes, she had never looked more beautiful. My father, handsome in his immaculate tuxedo, stood proudly by her side.

When we stepped into the tent, the space had been transformed into a glittering ballroom. All the tables and chairs were arranged in a semicircle around a large dance floor where the band was setting up their instruments. Crystal chandeliers hung down from wires, their soft white light reflecting on the faces of the people below, who were chatting and laughing, eager for the festivities to begin. My smile pasted on my face, I tried to enter into the celebratory mode, but all I could think about was how I might make a fast getaway. At long last it was time for dinner to begin. I sat down at my appointed seat and struggled to carry on a coherent conversation with my neighbor, a favorite cousin, who had flown in from the East for the occasion.

"Aren't you going to eat anything?" he asked.

"Not hungry," I replied. "Just a little nervous because I haven't been able to write a toast for my parents."

"Don't worry," he said. "You'll do fine."

That was just what Frank had told me. How I wished I could believe it. Then I saw my father step onto the dance floor and take the microphone. My breath caught in my throat.

"Welcome, everyone," he said, smiling broadly. "What a treat it is for my dear wife and me to welcome you here tonight from all over the country and abroad."

He waved to Barbara Ward, a treasured friend and world-famous economist, who had flown in from London the previous day. "And, of course, welcome to our beloved family. Will the grandchildren please come up so I can show you off?"

After he had introduced each one, several of them took turns in front of the microphone to make their toasts. The audience clapped heartily, clearly enjoying the love and respect the young people evidenced for their grandparents. Joining in the applause, I shuddered; thinking of the bleak contrast I would make if the best I could do was to repeat the pathetic effort I had made at my father's eightieth birthday back in June. My brother Wally got up next and read a poem he had written that was both humorous and touching. If only I could have come up with something like that.

"And now we will hear from my big sister, Titia," he declared as the applause died down.

I sat paralyzed, stuck to my chair. People began looking my way.

My cousin gave me a little pat and whispered, "Good luck."

Somehow I managed to lift myself up and make my way to the dance floor, where my brother handed me the microphone. I stared out over the sea of faces all gazing up at me expectantly.

When I opened my mouth to speak, no words emerged. A hush fell over the crowd.

Help me, dear God, I prayed inwardly.

There was another long silence. Then out from nowhere came a voice.

"Good evening, everyone," I heard it say calmly, and I realized with profound relief that it was coming from me. I had plunged in.

"How wonderful that we are all gathered here tonight to celebrate the momentous occasion of my parents' fiftieth anniversary. What an amazing achievement. Ann Landers, you should be taking notes for your advice to the lovelorn column."

I looked over at Ann, a close friend of my mother's, who was smiling broadly.

Laughter filled the tent. I laughed too, a surge of confidence running through me.

"But enough of that. It's time to let you all in on the inner workings of my parents' marriage. There are certain things only their daughter can tell you."

As I said this, I glanced down and saw my father's face stiffen. It flashed through my mind that I was dancing on thin ice. But there was no turning back now. The words seemed to be flowing on their own from some unknown source within my being.

"How have they made it work?" I asked. "After having done an in-depth study of their relationship, I believe the key to their success is that they have broken the rules society deems appropriate for husbands and wives. For example, instead of letting her spouse make the political decisions for them both, my mother worked tirelessly through two presidential campaigns for her political favorite, Adlai. My father, on the other hand, was steadfastly giving money and voting for his candidate, Ike. What is remarkable is that I never heard a harsh word spoken by either about this potentially explosive topic. In later years, it was the family joke that when election time came around, with one stroke of the pen, my parents neatly canceled out each other's vote."

I paused as laughter and some cheering filled the tent.

"My mother stood up for what she believed—a courageous act at home and in her social world. Need I point out that this woman is probably one of the few registered Democrats in this town? Treat her with respect.

"For me," I continued, my voice growing stronger, "it has taken becoming a psychologist and the support of the women's movement to understand how important it is that we women claim our right to be authentic and do what matters most to us instead of what the culture deems is proper. My mother is a tremendous role model for me in this. Her life is all the more impressive because she lived during a time when women weren't encouraged to make their mark out in the world or to further their own growth. When her work in the political arena was over, my mother decided to get a BA degree at the University of Chicago, something her mother had forbidden her to do as a girl. Those years of getting up at 6:00 AM to ride into Chicago on the early train for her 8:30 class could not have been easy, but she was so fired up over the plays of Shakespeare and the politics of the Federalists that nothing stopped her. I've thought of her often as I'm driving down to my classes at Northwestern during rush hour or in a snowstorm.

"All that time, my father was his wife's ardent supporter, never complaining about the amount of time she spent away at her work. But he didn't sit still either. After retiring from the family company, he surprised everyone by launching off in a challenging new direction—the restaurant business. Before long he had created, as most of you know, twelve incredible French restaurants that transformed the reputation of Chicago from a steak-and-potatoes town into a gourmet's paradise. I might add it was certainly a lot of fun for his children as well since he gave us the enviable job of hosting our friends from the suburbs at the opening of each new restaurant in the city. The best part was he picked up the bill. No wonder I never developed a flair in the kitchen!

"While my father's restaurants were thriving, my mother was appointed a delegate to the United Nations and rented an apartment in New York City. How we loved to visit her there and go to hear her speak before her fellow members at the assembly. I was privileged to meet many of her new friends, men in turbans, women in bright colored saris or other eye-catching dresses of their native lands—such fine people from emerging nations whose enthusiasm, intelligence, and caring for the world made a deep impression on me.

"When that era ended, my mother wasn't finished by a long shot. She sat down and began writing a book on the importance of volunteers in politics, a subject she was an expert on, having volunteered in at least six different campaigns. Since I have started writing my dissertation, I have even more respect for her drive and determination. I suspect she is going to get that book written and published well before I have finished mine.

"Now here we are tonight paying tribute to a remarkable and elegant couple who have made their marriage work and flourish by letting go of the roles that husbands and wives were supposed to play. Each of them set out to do the work they believed in, while at the same time they supported and respected the other. I would say that is what long-lasting love is all about."

I lowered the microphone and looked down at my parents.

"What a rich and wonderful life you have created. You have shared your gifts and your abundance freely with countless people, a large number of whom are here tonight to honor you. You have inspired me, your daughter, to live my own life to the fullest. I am grateful to you both for who you are, and—I thank you for picking me out forty-six years ago."

As I stepped down from the platform, people were standing and clapping. Some were wiping their eyes. I got back to my table in a daze, where my cousin greeted me with a big hug.

"I said you would do great," he declared.

I sat down in my chair, still overcome by the emotions that had filled me as I was speaking. Tears of gratitude came to my eyes as I took in, on an even deeper level, how blessed I was that these extraordinary people had chosen to adopt me and given me this life of bountiful opportunities. Even more important, I realized that all the judgment and hurt feelings I had carried for years had disappeared.

And yes, I felt worthy. Just as my mother, who had raised me and loved me, had stood up for her truth, so had I when I stood up and acknowledged in front of my parents and all their friends that I was adopted. In that moment I broke free of the secret and shed the stigma that had been the source of shame and insecurity throughout my life.

Later in the evening my mother came up to me and said, "Yours was the best of them all."

All through the night people had been congratulating me, but those few words from her were the ones that really mattered. They made my heart sing.

— 10 —

GREEN LIGHT

A WEEK AFTER MY parents' gala, I came across an article in the local paper titled "Mother Speaks with Love for Unseen, Unknown Son." I was amazed to discover that it was a letter written by a birth mother to her son, whom she had given up for adoption as an infant. Believe me, I had never, ever come across a personal story about adoption written from the birth mother's point of view. I read on avidly. That day was her son's eighteenth birthday. The mother told about the pain she still felt from never having had the chance to hold him, never being able to know if he was all right, how she thought of him every year at this time of his birth. She said she had written the adoption agency so that just in case he ever wanted to search, she would be happy to meet him. She ended with this advice:

"Tell your adoptive parents if you want to search. Ask them to help you; to work with you. They are your family. Then after you have learned about your birth parents, you will go back to your adopted family and I would let you go. You see, son, I do love you very much and I would still like to hold you."

Tears filled my eyes. My heart felt as if it were breaking apart. I had to wonder if this message was appearing just at this crucial moment to spur me on in my quest. Lord knows, I had been trying to convince myself to let go of the need to search for my birth mother and just be content, for goodness sake, with all the gratitude and love I was feeling toward my adoptive parents. But at that moment I saw more clearly than ever that the urgency to find the woman who had carried me in her womb had nothing to do with how positively I viewed the parents who chose me and raised me. This was a longing so deep that it affected every cell of my being.

I am well aware that not every adopted person experiences such powerful feelings, but it was true for me, and I had to follow that primal drive. Now there was a new possibility. My mother just might have this same urgency and want to find me as much as I yearned to find her.

I had to go outside and think about all this, so I called to Cola, the perfect companion—loving and true—and together we walked down the road to the park, a long, narrow stretch of grass that lay between the road and the big bluff overlooking Lake Michigan.

Sitting down on one of the wooden benches, I recalled how this place had often been a refuge for me, especially during the troubled times in my marriage when I would linger here for hours staring at the gray-blue water looking for answers. Today, the orange and yellow leaves on the towering elms whispered in the morning breeze. The sun moved out from behind a dark cloud, lighting the water below to a brilliant blue and warming my back. A feeling of peace flowed into me. My brain stopped agonizing over my birth mother, and I just let myself be immersed in the beauty around me.

Then it came to me—not as a voice, but as a knowing deep inside my being—that my birth mother was going to die within the year. If I waited to look for her until after I finished writing my dissertation, it would be too late. I felt amazingly calm as I took in this information. The next step was clear. I must send this article on to John MacGriffen, whom I hadn't heard from since he had sent me the photo of Keith James three months earlier. I said a prayer asking that his heart would open to me.

Fired with new purpose, I called to Cola and walked briskly home. Then I drove uptown to make a copy of the article, which I mailed to Mr. MacGriffen. I enclosed a brief note saying I hoped he could understand from the article why it might be beneficial for both my mother and me if I were to find her.

Late one night about a week later, Bill and I were reading in bed when the phone rang. I answered, and a familiar, gruff voice announced, "This is John MacGriffen."

My heart leapt into my throat.

"I got your letter," he said, "but I want you to know I had already decided to give you the information you requested. My only consideration was for the young people involved."

"I understand that," I replied. "I plan to be very careful."

"I hope so. Her name is Dorie Phelps, and she came from Vermont. That's all I know about her."

"Thank you," I said, hardly able to breathe.

"I have not been well this summer," he continued.

"Is it your heart?"

"No, other things. But my children are monitoring my mail. It would be best if you did not write again."

"I will respect your wishes."

"Good. Good-bye."

"Good-bye, and thank you again. I am grateful."

The line went dead.

I hung up the phone, awash in feelings.

"I know her name," I told Bill. "It's Dorie Phelps."

"That's great news," he responded excitedly.

"Yes, it is, but I must admit," I added, "I also feel a little sad because John MacGriffen told me not to contact him again. How I hoped he would like me, whether he was my father or not."

"I know you did. But don't forget he just gave you what you most wanted."

"You're right," I conceded. "I'm not going to let his rejection get me down. This is a moment to celebrate. I know my mother's name."

As I said that, I jumped out of bed and whirled around the room, calling, "Dorie Phelps, I'm coming. I'm coming."

"But remember," Bill cautioned, "you only have her name so far. Finding her may be a different matter."

"I'm not worried; I'm sure I'm going to be with her soon. I have to be. Time is short."

*   *   *

Early the next morning, I followed the advice of a friend, who was a genealogist, and called the archival department in Montpelier, the capital of Vermont. A pleasant-sounding man answered. "Sam Johnson here. What can I do for you?"

"I'm looking for a Dorie Phelps," I told him, after introducing myself. "She was born somewhere in Vermont around 1910. Do you think you can help me?"

"Probably," drawled the voice on the other end of the line. "Why are you looking for her?"

Oops. I wasn't prepared to answer his question. What would he think if he knew the truth? "Well, uh," I stammered, "she's important to me. She's my mother."

"Your mother? You're trying to find your mother. How did you lose her?"

I had done it now. All I could do was be honest. "You see, I was adopted as a baby. I am forty-six years old now, and I want to find my birth mother."

A long pause followed. Would he help me, or would he say I had no right to be doing this?

"Well, isn't that something?" he replied. "I never had anyone ask me for help in a matter like this before. But I guess it's okay. You're old enough to know what you're doing."

I exhaled a huge breath. "Thank you."

"Let me check this out for you. If you give me your address, I'll write to you about what I discover," my new cohort offered.

"Oh, I couldn't possibly wait that long. What if I call you back tomorrow morning?"

"That's fine. Hope I have some good news for you."

I hung up, my heart racing. This was my first conversation with someone who worked for the state of Vermont in an official capacity. What a good plainspoken man, such a change from the majority of bureaucrats whom I had dealt with previously. It seemed my luck was taking a turn for the better.

The next day I had to drive into Chicago for my small group meeting at the Family Institute where I was studying to become a specialist in marital and family therapy. Our current topic, fittingly enough, was about which had more effect on our development: nature or nurture. These kinds of discussions were always challenging for me since I had no idea from whom I had inherited what.

Now all that was going to change. I was about to find out who my ancestors were, those ghosts whose DNA flowed in my cellular and emotional bodies, and made me who I was.

Isn't this perfect timing, I thought as I dialed Sam Johnson's number just before class from the pay phone out in the hall. One of my instructors from the previous year strolled by and asked, "How's your search coming?"

"I may be finding out about my birth mother and her family in this very phone call," I told her excitedly.

"That's wonderful," she said, "but remember no matter what you discover, it's the process you're going through that's important, even more than the outcome."

Her reply didn't make much sense to me, fixated on the goal as I was, but I tucked it away in a corner of my brain for further thought. Then Sam answered and I forgot about everything else.

"I've found her," he announced, his voice jubilant. "Doris Ella Phelps, born March, 30, 1909, in Milton, Vermont. Her parents are Ethel Benham Phelps and Karl Phelps. They're both dead, so I looked for their obituaries in the Burlington Free Press. I only found Ethel's, who died in 1946, but it said she was survived by her husband, two sons, Julian and Benham, and a third child, Mrs. Doris Horr of Malweh, New York."

I was overwhelmed. This man had discovered more than I'd even thought to ask for. Not only did I now know the town where my mother had been born, but I knew what her married name was and where she was living, at least back in 1946. As well, he'd given me the names of all her immediate family. I thanked him profusely, but he demurred, saying he still had more investigating to do.

"I want to find out when your grandfather died. Then we will know much more. This is more exciting than a mystery story."

*   *   *

Once again the time had come to relate another new and possibly quite threatening development to my adoptive parents. Now it could be my mother who would be upset since I was zeroing in on my birth mother. If that happened, would my father become angry and attempt to protect her?

I walked into their house the next morning and greeted my parents, who were finishing up their breakfast at the dining room table. Anxious to get this over with as soon as possible, I moved quickly to the point of my visit.

"Mr. MacGriffen called me Sunday. He gave me my birth mother's name and said she lived in Vermont. Later I talked to a man who works in the Vermont archives. He found out her married name and who her parents were."

I paused, scarcely able to breathe.

"I see," said my mother calmly. "And what is her maiden name?"

"Doris Phelps," I replied, taken aback by my mother's serene demeanor.

"Phelps," my mother repeated thoughtfully. "That name sounds familiar. When you first told me about Mr. MacGriffen, I didn't recognize that name at all, but I didn't want to stop you or discourage you. But Phelps," she said, "yes, that was the name on your birth records."

I could scarcely believe what I was hearing. My adoptive mother was confirming that Doris Phelps was indeed my birth mother.

"Thanks, Mom," I said. "I appreciate you telling me that."

My father, as usual, sat there silent. Nothing surprising about that. He had never said anything about my toast at the anniversary party either. I thought about asking him what he felt but decided against it. Why open up Pandora's box again? That, I realized later, was a mistake. Back then, I was only just starting to understand that every time I was honest with my parents and also gave them the opportunity to share their feelings no matter how painful or difficult those might be, we all became stronger and more real.

Then my mother said, "We've received so many thank-you letters since the party. A good number of our friends mentioned your toast as one of the highlights. Eppie loved not only what you said about her but also your last words."

Inwardly I chuckled. Eppie Lederer was the real name of Ann Landers, the author of an advice column for the *Chicago Sun-Times*, who became my nemesis when she had written in one of her columns that it was wrong for adoptees to search for their birth parents. My mother had triumphantly quoted her words to me when she was trying to dissuade me from my quest.

Now that the advice maven's words no longer mattered, I just smiled and said, "That's nice to hear."

But she wasn't finished.

"I was on the phone with another guest, Charlie Saxton, yesterday. He mentioned how much your toast meant to him. Then he told me all about his own children who were adopted."

Charlie was a respected friend as well as CEO of a Fortune 500 company. If he approved of my talking about being adopted in public and then did so himself, that would help my mother become more comfortable with the topic. It seemed that my toast was having a ripple effect among her community. I had taken the taboo subject out of the closet and made it okay to discuss in the world.

My mother walked me to the front door, holding tightly onto my arm. "Please keep me informed about what you discover next."

"I promise I will. Always remember that I love you. The truth is, I believe this search—hard as it's been at times for both of us—has brought us closer."

She was silent a moment. Then she nodded. "You know, you may be right about that."

I couldn't resist.

"So maybe Eppie was off base in her advice after all," I added, giving her a wink.

My mother actually giggled. "That could be," she admitted.

When I left her, I ran across the lawn to our home, my heart pounding with excitement.

"Bill," I called as I barreled through the back door and came upon him sitting on the couch reading the newspaper. "My mother confirmed that Phelps is the name on my birth records. Isn't it incredible she did that?"

"That's it," he said, throwing down the paper, "That's just what you needed to hear. I was worried that you didn't have enough facts to be sure Doris Phelps was your birth mom. Mr. MacGriffen's story could have been fabricated to throw you off the trail. But now your mother has given you the proof you need to go ahead."

"I never doubted," I replied, "that he had told me the truth. And now to think that my adoptive mother was able to calmly corroborate his words."

I shook my head in wonder.

"She has traveled a long way to meet me on this journey. It just makes me love her even more."

— 11 —

ROLLER-COASTER RIDE

Now that I knew my mother's married name, Bill and I went off to the Chicago Public Library to look up Horr in the current phone books on file for all the states. I soon realized how lucky I was that, as with Mr. MacGriffen, my mother had married a man with an unusual name. Naturally the place to begin was in the town of Malweh, New York, but Doris Horr was no longer there. Broadening our search, we looked through all the phone books in New York state, then throughout New England, and ended up discovering eleven people with the name Horr.

Even though I felt the old urge pushing me to begin going down the list calling each name, this time I controlled myself. I stopped in my tracks with my mother only a phone call away. It was pretty clear that my headlong approach had alienated and frightened the MacGriffens, although I sincerely doubt that John MacGriffen would have welcomed me even if I had been more discreet. Now I had to face the possibility that my mother might not want to know me either. Not that she could deny being my mother—I had too much proof for that. But most likely she would not have told her husband about me. My appearance—revealing the shameful secret of her past—could shatter her marriage. The thought that my birth mother might reject me a second time was too painful to contemplate.

One risk I never considered was the possibility that my mother might be an unsavory character whom I wouldn't want to claim. I always believed in her inherent goodness. That was one of the most important things I wanted to tell her when we were finally reunited. And here is a weird thing. As a child, I had always thought that somehow my birth mother's abandonment of me was my fault. If only I had been more lovable, she wouldn't have let me go. If I could have prevented my birth mother's abandoning me by being a better daughter, then I would work really hard to be more lovable the second time around so my new adoptive mother would want to keep me. And believe me, I had tried.

Right now, I was in a quandary over what was the best way to approach my birth mother. I didn't know how to deal with all my feelings, which were in turmoil, so I retreated—as I knew how to do so well—into my mind. I arranged to meet with Cynthia, my genealogist friend, at the Newberry Library in Chicago with the intention of looking up everyone in my mother's background. By this time, my new friend, Sam from Montpelier, had sent me my grandfather Karl Phelps's obituary, which stated that Karl had been associated with his father in running a general store and an insurance business and was survived by two sons, Benham and Julian, and a daughter, Mrs. William (Doris) Horr.

In the list of people that we had compiled from the telephone books, there were three William Horrs, two of whom were in New York and one in South Hero, Vermont.

I had a distinct feeling that the one in Vermont was my mother.

*   *   *

The next day, Cynthia and I had a most satisfying visit to the library. We zeroed in on Orville Guy Phelps, born in 1834, who had a resume that would knock the socks off any reasonably hardworking person unless he happened to be a fellow Vermonter. O. G. was not only a farmer (the owner of fifteen dairy cows) and a produce dealer but also a life and fire insurance agent. Additionally, he was an agent for agricultural implements and dairying apparatus. In his spare time, he sold sugar evaporators in Bellows Falls and managed to produce five children. His fifth child was Karl Julian Phelps, my grandfather. We also discovered a small book about the whole Phelps family, which told how they were leaders in Dorchester, Massachusetts, before moving to

Windsor, Connecticut, then on to South Hero, Vermont, and finally settling in Milton, Vermont.

Now I knew for sure that my mother was in South Hero. We looked it up on the map and discovered that it was a small town on an island in Lake Champlain, right across the water from Milton.

Cynthia showed me how to make my family tree. Beginning with my mother, Doris Ella Phelps, born in Milton, Vermont, on July 30, 1909, to Ethel Benham Phelps and Karl Phelps, I traced her ancestors all the way back to William Phelps, who left his home in Tewkesbury, Gloucestershire, England, to sail from Plymouth, England, to Nantasket, Massachusetts, in 1630 on the ship *The John and Mary*. My grandmother's family, John Benham and his sons, came over on the same ship. There went my childhood fantasy of having Russian parents. I was English through and through on this side of the family. Only my mother could tell me where the other side of the family was from.

When I returned home, I felt exhilarated yet strangely calm. After wondering all my life about where I came from, I finally had my family tree. I knew my history on my mother's side, and I loved it. What brave, adventurous people the Phelpses were, making their way over from England and eventually settling in the rugged land of Vermont, where they worked hard and prospered. I came from good, solid stock. I was ready to call my mother and reveal that I had found her, and that I was proud to be part of her rich heritage.

I told Bill I was going to phone her in the morning, but before I did, there was one last piece of preparation I needed to do. Jeanie, my very first and closest childhood friend, had just returned from her family's summer cottage in—where else—Vermont. When I had filled her in on the latest developments in my search, she urged me to call the town clerk in South Hero before contacting my mother. She explained that since these people know everyone and everything that happens in their towns, there might be some information about my mother that would help me when I talked to her.

That night I lay awake for hours, going over in my mind what I wanted to say to my birth mother. First, I would disclose that I had something very personal to discuss with her and ask if she were alone. After that, I would tell her I had been researching my family history and believed we were related. Hopefully, she would be curious and want to know more. The big giveaway would come next. I would tell her that

I was born on May 9, 1934. If she didn't respond to that, I would go the final step and announce I was her long-lost daughter.

I tried out my speech on Bill the next morning as he was having breakfast. I was in such a state of flux that I couldn't eat a thing.

"Do you think it's all right?' I asked anxiously. "Am I coming on too strong?"

"I don't know how you can be subtle when you're telling someone you've never met before that you are her daughter," my husband replied reasonably. "It's fine. Do you want me here when you call?"

"Thanks, I appreciate your offering, but I do better with these difficult things when I'm on my own."

After Bill drove off, I made myself a cup of tea, hoping it would soothe my stomach. The clock on the stove said 10:00 AM. This was as good a time as any. I went up to my bedroom and sat quietly in my chair for several minutes, praying for guidance. It felt right that I was going to talk to the town clerk in South Hero first. I guessed I needed a few more minutes to get ready for the most momentous phone call of my whole life. Then I picked up the receiver, found the number from Information, and dialed.

To my dismay, the town clerk had never heard of Doris Phelps Horr.

"I'll go in the back," she said, "and check the records, just to be sure."

I waited, fingers clenched around the receiver.

A minute later she returned. "Yes, now I remember her. The Phelps part confused me. I found Doris P. Horr, but she no longer lives in South Hero," she reported cheerily.

Oh no, I groaned inwardly, *here we go again.*

"But I know where she is," she added.

"Where?" I said, hope rising.

"She's down in a nursing home in Florida, totally incompetent."

Incompetent? What in God's name did she mean by that?

"Are you saying she's senile?" I managed to ask, my heart pounding.

"Yes, I remember her now. I don't think she even knows who her husband is anymore. It's a shame. She was such a lovely person."

The town clerk rattled on, unaware of the shock waves her words were producing in me.

"She's been this way for several years. I hear Bill Horr is still in town packing up to go back down to Florida to his winter home."

"Where does Bill live in Florida?" I asked through the fog that had descended around me.

"I think it's Venice."

I made myself thank her and slowly hung up the phone. I sat there in the chair holding on to the arms for dear life.

How could this be? My mother senile? She didn't even know her own husband. How would she ever know me?

The ringing of the telephone roused me. Automatically I picked it up and said hello.

"Are you all right? Your voice sounds awful."

It was Joan.

"No, I'm not all right. I just found out my birth mother is senile."

"It can't be true," she gasped. "After all your work to find her. It's too awful."

"I know. I can't talk now. Call me later."

I continued to sit in the chair, staring out at nothing. By now I was numb. I lost all track of time.

At some point I took a walk with Cola, but it didn't lift the heaviness pressing down on my heart. Later I tried to eat, but the sandwich tasted like sawdust. Finally I went back upstairs to sit in my chair and wait until Bill came home. My journal was on the table beside my chair. It was usually such a comfort to write my feelings and thoughts in it, but I didn't have the strength to pick it up. There was nothing to do but sit. And wait.

Naturally my mind went into the "if onlys." If only I hadn't given up on my search for two years after I received that first upsetting letter from Spence. And how different it would have been if only my parents had given me my birth records when I had first asked for them three and a half years ago. Even more painful, my adoptive mother had known my mother's name was Phelps all this time. I wished I had asked her again at a later date if she knew the name, but would she have told me?

If I had found my birth mother a few years earlier, might she have known me? Now it was too late. I would never be able to tell her that

I had always loved her and ask if she loved me. I would never find out who my father was.

I got up and went into the bathroom and looked in the mirror. My face was gaunt and haggard. Was this my mother's face staring back at me? Would I ever see her now? It felt as if she were already dead.

When Bill returned, he found me in my chair in the darkening room.

"What's wrong? Are you okay?"

"No," I replied and told him what I had discovered.

"What can I do?" he asked.

"I think," I said tentatively, "that I would like you to hold me."

"Come here then," he responded, gently pulling me to my feet. My body was so rigid that I could hardly walk. He led me over to the bed, eased me down, and lay beside me. When I felt his strong arms go around me, something in me let go, and I began to sob.

∗   ∗   ∗

A while later Bill reminded me apologetically that he had to leave to teach his business class. I wandered around the house in a dazed state, not knowing what to do with myself. All my systems seemed to have shut down.

The phone rang. I didn't want to deal with whoever was on the line, but the ringing was so insistent that I finally answered.

It was Corson, my brother-in-law.

"Listen, Titia, Joan's told me about your mother being totally out of it." I flinched hearing her described that way. "It's such a shock. But we feel you shouldn't give up now. Why don't you call Dorie's husband and ask him for the phone numbers of her brothers? After all, they knew about you."

My whole body recoiled. I couldn't think of any response.

Joan got on the line. "I feel awful even talking about Corson's idea when you must be so down," she said. "But think about it. At least if you contacted her brothers, you could find out more about your poor mother."

"I just can't imagine doing such a thing. I feel as if all the life has been drained out of me. But thanks for your caring anyway."

I hung up and went back upstairs to sit in the chair. What good would it do to talk to those men? I wanted my mother! She was the one I wanted to love me. Now I would never see her. The pain in my heart was insistent. The only thing I could think of doing was crawling into bed, pulling the covers around me, and sleeping for a long time.

Yet even though I was exhausted, sleep wouldn't come. My brain was bombarding me. *It's over; it's over.* All my work, time, and energy were for nothing. What a disaster this search had turned out to be. The man my mother claimed was my father had rejected the position. The man she was in love with was killed in an accident twenty years ago. My mother, the person I wanted the most, was senile.

It was time to give it all up. My adoptive parents would be pleased with that decision. Bill would be relieved as well. I certainly was no joy to live with these days, totally preoccupied with my quest that nothing else seemed to matter. My mood swings were so wild that I could hardly weather them myself.

Just as I was feeling clear about my decision, a small voice inside me whispered, *There is another side. You have done all this work. Why give up everything now?*

I couldn't believe I was hearing correctly. This was crazy. It was obvious there was no point left in searching. Hadn't all the key people dropped out of the picture?

Wait a minute, the voice continued. *You could get in touch with your uncles and find out more about your mother. They were the ones who took her in when she was pregnant with you. They can tell you, just as well as your mother could, about your whole birth family. You still want to know about them, don't you? Besides, they could show you pictures of your mother.*

There might not be much time, persisted the voice. *These men are older than Dorie. Don't pass this opportunity up when you are so close. You'll never forgive yourself.*

I sat up in bed. Maybe this wasn't such an absurd idea after all. Why couldn't I call Bill Horr and ask him to give me the phone numbers of my uncles? Getting out of bed, I stumbled in the dark over to my chair and sat down. I asked God to let me know if I was harming anyone by this new plan. I waited a while, but no clear answer came. But I couldn't help noticing that somehow my despair seemed less overwhelming.

My mind was starting to gear up in that old familiar way. What could I tell Bill Horr that wouldn't give away who I was? Why not just say I was researching my ancestral line and found I was a second cousin of Dorie's mother? That was far enough removed to keep him from suspecting anything.

The more I let my imagination play, the clearer it became that I really could do this. I turned on the light, reached for the phone, and called information in South Hero for his number, my mother's number. But this was a far different kind of call than I had been planning to make many hours ago. What was there to risk any longer? I had already lost her. I dialed the number.

A cheerful voice answered, "Bill Horr here."

I decided to make myself be upbeat in return.

"Hello, this is Titia Ellis, calling from Illinois. You don't know me, but I've been researching my family tree and find I may be related to your wife's side of the family. I'm wondering if you could connect me with her brothers who can give me more information. And I'm suddenly realizing I'm calling you awfully late."

"No problem," he said reassuringly. "Benham died in 1960, but Julian is still alive. In fact, he would be a good person to talk to. He's also interested in all the ancestors. Just a minute, I'll get his address for you."

My heart was pounding. Was it going to be this easy after all my trials? Bill Horr seemed to be such a trusting person that I was taken aback.

"Here is Julian's address," he said giving me the details.

Then came the question I'd been waiting for.

"What relation are you looking up, by the way?"

I tried to sound casual but convincing. "I'm a second cousin of Ethel Phelps."

"Oh, that would be my wife's mother. And how did you find me?"

"Well, I got hold of Karl Phelps's obituary and it mentioned a daughter, Mrs. William Horr in South Hero. I called the town clerk to get the number. She said your wife was in a nursing home."

"Yes, she's been there for two years."

"I'm sorry to hear that," I said. If he only knew how sorry! "Thank you for your help."

"Julian should be able to give you all the information you need. Good luck."

I hung up, filled with hope and new energy. There was no thought of going back to bed. Before this phone call, I had been so down I could have easily given up on my search or at least delayed for months. By that time, Bill Horr or Julian might have died. Now a new path had opened up. I no longer felt powerless. Contacting Dorie's brother wouldn't be betraying anyone. He was the one person left in the world who already knew about me. I could hardly wait for morning to come to call up this new character in the ongoing drama.

When Bill returned a short time later, I was eager to fill him in on what I had done since he left. His reaction was not encouraging.

"I can't believe it," he said in exasperation. "You've already called Bill Horr? And now you are going to get a hold of this brother. You never give up, do you? All you ever think about is this obsession with finding your birth family. I miss you. Will this search ever end, so we can get back to our life together?"

"Not until I see my mother," I heard myself saying. That was a surprise. I hadn't known till that moment that I had to see her, no matter what condition she was in.

And, of course, my poor husband had every right to be sick of this whole journey. I couldn't have stood me if I were he. But I wasn't; I was totally driven me, and I would press on leaving no clue unexplored, no possible relative safe from my need to know the truth. Probably there was no one else who could understand this driving need to find the answers to my past unless they too were adopted.

— 12 —

ACKNOWLEDGED AT LAST

THE FOLLOWING MORNING AFTER enjoying a real breakfast, I wrote out what I wanted to say to Julian Phelps. It wasn't that hard because at last I could be honest about who I was. Bill had already left, muttering "good luck" as he went out the back door. I went into the den, asked God to be with me, and made my call.

He answered after the first ring. "This is Julian."

I took a deep breath.

"You don't know me," I began, "but I have something personal to tell you. Is this a good time to talk?"

I waited breathlessly. A guarded "yes" came over the line.

I told him who I was, about being adopted from Spence, and all that I had discovered right down to my birth mother's two brothers who helped her when she was pregnant with me.

Finally I came to the end of my story and waited for him to reply, perspiration soaking my shirt. There was a long silence.

Finally the disembodied voice said, "I haven't talked about this with anyone since it happened, not even my wife who is dead now."

He was admitting everything. Relief flowed through me.

"I phoned Bill Horr to get your phone number and address."

There was no response on the other end of the line—just an ocean of quiet. I heard myself babbling on and stopped, saying, "This is a difficult conversation, isn't it?"

He actually chuckled. "Yes, it is."

Gathering up my courage, I continued. "I would love to see any pictures that you have of my mother and her family."

"I don't have any pictures," Julian Phelps replied quickly.

"I was hoping I might come see you and talk about my mother," I persisted. "I was devastated to learn she is in a nursing home."

"She's completely senile," he said. "She didn't know me the last time I saw her."

I decided to drop the talk of visiting him since he hadn't picked up on it. Instead I began telling him about my research into the family history at the Newberry Library. He was surprised to hear how much I had learned. When I told him about discovering the Phelps family book, he replied that he had one too and that it was dog-eared. Inwardly, I thanked myself, or whatever was guiding me, for deciding to do all that research on my ancestors before I called. It wouldn't have made a bit of difference to my mother because our relationship would have been all about the heart, but it turned out to be a valuable asset in helping me connect with her brother.

"Does Bill Horr know that Dorie had me?" I dared ask finally, trying to keep my voice from shaking.

"Yes, he does. Doris told him before they got married."

Some of my tension lifted. What a brave thing for my mother to have done.

"I'm glad she told him and glad he married her anyway. Would you mind telling me if she had any other children after her marriage?"

Another silence.

"You don't have to tell me their names," I added hurriedly, "just their sex and age."

"She had some daughters who are in their thirties," he said briefly.

I have sisters! I loved thinking about that.

"I'd like to come talk to you and see some photos," I told him again.

"Well, I might have some photos," he admitted. "Tell me your address and I'll send them to you."

Poor man, he didn't know who he was dealing with—a woman desperate to learn the truth who wasn't going to let him get off that easily.

"My husband and I are coming east in two weeks to see our daughter at college. We could stop by and see you then."

No reply.

"Why don't I give you some time to think about all this, and I'll call you at the beginning of the week."

He agreed. We said good-bye and hung up.

My hand was shaking as I put down the receiver. This had not been an effortless phone call. Julian Phelps had admitted he was my mother's brother, but he understandably wasn't altogether welcoming of the illegitimate daughter wanting to return to the fold. Like John MacGriffen, could he have feared I might "want vengeance"?

I sat down and wrote my very best mollifying letter saying I hoped he wasn't too upset by my call and tried to explain why it was important to me to know who my birth family was. I gave the requisite background on my adoptive parents, told about Bill's and my own family, and included a photo that had been taken of us all at our niece's wedding at Middlebury, Vermont, this past summer. I ended by saying I would call next week just before we were coming east to see if he would be willing to meet with us.

After I mailed the letter, the waiting began. But even as I started on a whole new chapter with my uncle, I couldn't stop the tears that flowed every time I thought about my mother and felt the anguish of having missed my chance to be with her. Each task required an enormous effort. It was all I could do to try to be present with my clients. At home I was moody and snapped at my long-suffering husband. More than anything I just wanted to hole up in my room and retreat from the world.

*   *   *

The following Monday I pulled myself together as best I could and called Julian Phelps. "Did you get my letter?" I asked, my stomach doing flip-flops.

"Yes, yes, I did," said the voice on the other end of the line.

I waited—a long time.

At last I said, "I was hoping my husband and I could come and see you this Thursday."

"Just a minute. Let me check my calendar."

Another long pause. I forgot to breathe.

"Well, yes," he conceded abruptly. "It happens I am free all day Thursday."

I could hardly hold on to the phone, my hand was shaking so badly.

Then he gave me a long, involved description of how to find his house.

When he was finally finished, I said, "I'm grateful you've agreed to see me. And I'm really looking forward to our meeting."

"I am too," responded my new uncle, much to my surprised delight.

After hanging up the phone, I ran up the stairs to our bedroom where Bill was getting dressed and announced, "Julian Phelps is going to see us. My blood uncle said he is looking forward to meeting me. Can you believe it?"

Tears filled my eyes. "Even though I found my mother too late, still I'm being acknowledged, illegitimate and all. On top of that, I'm being given the opportunity to take the first step into my birth family's circle."

I sat down on the bed. "Well, I did pull out all the stops to get that invitation. Julian certainly wasn't going to ask me to walk into his living room on his own. I can't say I blame him."

"I'm sure your letter to him helped," Bill replied. "Now maybe you can relax a little."

"I feel like a yo-yo these days. I have been so devastated about my mother, then moving from that to trying to persuade her brother to let me come see him. I know I haven't been easy to live with."

"That's for sure," Bill said. "I never knew this search of yours would be all-consuming."

"Neither did I, but I can't stop now." A foreboding quiver ran through me. "I hope you can hang in there with me until I see this through."

"I'm doing my best, but you're asking a lot." His voice became edgy. "You just go ahead doing what you want. It's obvious you don't care about me and my needs. Look at our house. It's a mess! Do I have to do everything?"

I jumped into the fray with all systems on red alert.

"Don't you understand that this search is the most important thing in my life right now? I haven't any energy left to deal with your needs. And who cares about how clean our house looks!"

Oh dear, I knew those words were going to be trouble the minute they came flying out of my mouth. Bill was really angry now. I responded in kind. Finally he turned and rushed out of the room, banging the door behind him. I followed, telling him to come back so we could resolve this, but he was already out in the garage getting into his car to drive off.

I went back and collapsed upon the bed, berating myself for being so obsessed with what mattered to me that I had taken him for granted. As for the mess, it was true that I wasn't about to win the *Good Housekeeping* award for cleanliness. I just didn't notice the stuff lying around that drove him crazy. This had been the cause of many explosions over the years. And Bill's anger was frightening. Whenever he blew up, I was sure it meant he didn't love me anymore. Even more frightening was his withdrawal afterward. Did it mean that some day he would never come back?

I remember telling a psychologist once how threatened I felt when Bill retreated. His response was, "Are you really that afraid you can't hold on to your man?"

Naturally I felt foolish and pathetic, but at this point I see why I was terrified. If I couldn't hold on to the mother who had nurtured me in her womb, why would I think I'd be able to keep my beloved husband? This lifelong fear of abandonment made me feel yucky about myself. I tried to keep it hidden, but I knew it often hindered me from going out on my own or from encouraging Bill to do the same. Now because my passion to find my mother overrode my dependence, I was beginning to follow my own course. But that didn't mean that I was healed of my fear of losing him.

*   *   *

When Bill returned that evening, I went literally weak with relief, no matter that he looked grim and forbidding. As always, wanting to do whatever I possibly could to re-establish a connection, I rushed into apologies, but he shook his head.

"I don't want to talk about it."

That night we tossed and turned in bed, each clinging to the edge of our side of the mattress. Somehow I got through the next day seeing clients at the office. I even made headway on the housework, trying to keep busy so I wouldn't think about the fact that we were supposed to be flying out in a few days to see Julian Phelps. Would I end up doing that on my own?

Over dinner, Bill finally broke through the wall of silence. "I'm coming back. It just takes me a long time after we fight. I feel awful about myself when I get so angry, but I can't control it."

"I'm sorry I've been so hung up on my birth mother that I haven't paid attention to you," I replied. "And you're right. The house was a mess."

"Thanks for saying that and for cleaning up. I know that a neat house means more to me than it does to you. I just feel you don't care about me when you let everything go."

The strain between us began to ease. By the time we had finished eating, we were discussing our forthcoming trip to see my uncle.

*   *   *

On the plane flying east, I turned to Bill. "I want to make a connection with Julian and get some answers, but he was pretty guarded on the phone. At least he's not angry and threatened like John MacGriffen was."

Once we landed, it didn't take long to rent our car and, following Julian's directions, make our way to his home. The door opened before we had even rung the bell. He had been watching for us.

I was face to face with the first person in my birth family who actually acknowledged being related to me. He was such a formidable personality on the phone, but here was a little man not much taller than I. His round face was encircled by a thinning thatch of gray and a trim little beard, accented with a mustache and bushy brown eyebrows that hung over his glasses.

"Come in, come in," Julian said eagerly as he ushered us into the sunny living room filled with comfortable furniture grouped around a brick fireplace.

He looked straight at Bill. "I recognize you from the picture."

My body went slack. Was he going to ignore me the way John MacGriffen had for the first half hour of our visit?

At that moment, Julian turned to face me. "By the way, I found a few family pictures. Would you like to see them?"

I almost jumped in my enthusiasm. "I would love to."

"Please make yourselves comfortable," he said, gesturing to the gray sofa. Then he went over to the bureau and picked up some loose photos.

"Here is a picture of the general store in Milton," he said giving me a small, black and white photo. "You can see the sign over the door saying 'O. G. Phelps.' This was taken in 1922 when Teddy Roosevelt came to town. That's why the area outside the front of the store is jammed with people."

With trembling hands, I held the photo, my first view of my history.

"I love that my grandfather owned a general store, and how incredible that the president visited there. Do you have any photos of the inside?"

Julian shook his head. "Afraid not."

Then, without preamble, he asked, "Would you like to see a picture of Doris?"

I nodded, suddenly unable to speak.

He handed me another photo two by three inches in size, curling around the edges. Then he sat down on the couch beside me. "Here we are out in the canoe on Lake Champlain," he explained, leaning over to point. "That's me sitting next to Doris in the bottom of the boat, and our older brother, Benham, is sitting up behind us."

My heart pounding, I stared at the picture of my mother. She looked about eighteen, and she was leaning back with one foot up on the canoe thwart. She must be short because her head barely came up to Julian's shoulder. Her body seemed relaxed, and she was dressed casually in a striped shirt and a pair of shorts. I couldn't really see her eyes as she was smiling down at something. I felt grateful when Julian got up to look for more photos. I needed more time to take all this in.

I am forty-six years old, and this is my first glimpse of my mother. Do I look like her? We both had dark, short, curly hair, dark eyebrows, and large mouths, but there was no shock of recognition. I had waited all my life to discover who I looked like in my birth family. Since I hadn't resembled John MacGriffen (the man I still wanted to believe was my father despite his protests to the contrary) or his daughter, I had felt sure I would look just like my mother. She was the one I hoped to take after. But I couldn't find what my heart was aching to see.

Studying my mother further, I had to admit that no matter how disappointed I was, I loved how she looked. I wanted to drink her in like a tall glass of water. She was not only pretty but also completely at ease and natural in that canoe, and wearing shorts! That was quite a cool thing to be doing back in the late 1920s. She also seemed innocent and carefree.

Little did she know then what life had in store for her—that in a few years she would have a baby girl by a man she didn't love and then have to give her up. What had that been like for her? Had she been able to forget me and go on with her life? I hoped that wasn't the case. All of a sudden I had the yearning to bring the photo up to my lips and kiss her.

Julian came back at this moment bringing over more black and white photos, all obviously pulled out of an album. "Here are all our children," he said, giving me another small photo showing seven young people sitting in a row on a porch stoop. "There are Benham's three— those two girls and a boy—then Doris's two girls, and my two sons."

I gazed at my two half-sisters who were probably in their teens. They looked attractive and fun, one dark haired, the other blond, but once again, I didn't seem to resemble either of them. Was there anyone out there who looked like me? I wondered if I might ever get to meet my half-sisters. Would we be friends some day? I hadn't even thought about this before, but now that I didn't have much hope of establishing a relationship with my mother, they were the next closest relatives. Having sisters seemed even more important since I had lost Leslie, the sister I had grown up with.

"Here's a picture of my parents," Julian said, breaking into my reflections and handing me a photo of an older man and woman standing close together, staring straight into the camera.

These are my grandparents, I thought excitedly. *They are my lineage.* I liked my grandfather immediately. He was a solid-looking man in a casual, long-sleeved work shirt. He had gray hair, a lot more of it than Julian. His eyes were kind behind his glasses, and his smile gentle. He looked a little sad. My grandmother was plump, her gray hair pulled back in a bun. She too wore glasses and had a half smile. Despite her simple cotton dress, she conveyed dignity and strength.

"They look just the way I would have wanted them to," I pronounced happily.

"Here," said Julian, handing me two photos. "You can have these pictures of Doris and us in the rowboat and this one of the general store. I'll make copies of the others and send them to you if you'd like."

I was thrilled. "Thanks, that's very kind of you."

Julian checked his watch and announced it was time to go to lunch. He drove us to a roadhouse about half a mile away. Inside the big room we were greeted by noisy chattering, but as soon as we sat down at our brown wooden table, all I heard was the conversation with my uncle. He was glad to answer all my questions about his life and his parents. The only difficulty came when I tried to get a clearer picture of what my mother was like. Every time I asked something about her, his responses were short and provided little detail.

He said she had always been cheerful and not a very good student, particularly in analytical geometry.

"I just about failed geometry in high school," I inserted, feeling inordinately pleased that we shared this shortcoming.

"I used to help her with her homework," Julian continued.

"Did you and she play together as kids?"

"I don't remember much playing back then," he said, shrugging his shoulders. "I went off to college when she was pretty young."

"How about when she got older?" I asked

"Doris attended the University of Vermont for two years. When money became tight, she left and went down to Boston to get a job as a secretary. We hardly ever saw each other. That's really all there was to it."

I decided to take the plunge and find out the truth about my father.

"They told me at Spence that she fell in love with a medical student who jilted her. When she turned to his best friend for support, I was conceived. Did she ever talk to you about that?"

"Never," he said adamantly, his face set in a grimace.

"But she must have said something or you and the lawyer wouldn't have gone up to Boston to see John MacGriffen," I persevered. Oh, dear,

I hoped I wasn't squandering the good will Julian had shown toward me by closing in like this, but I had to know what really happened.

"It was my brother who did that. I don't know anything about it."

"Mr. MacGriffen told me he came down and met with my mother after I was born, that she became hysterical," I persisted. By now I felt like I was trying to catch hold of a fish that continually slipped out of my grasp.

"No, I don't remember that." Julian said.

Finally I stopped myself. It was fairly obvious even to me that this approach wasn't working. Taking a big breath, I tried a different tact.

"I feel badly to be asking you all these questions, but I need to know the truth. John MacGriffen denied he was my father when I went to see him. Now that my mother is senile and your brother has died, you are the only person who can tell me whether he really is my father."

Julian met my gaze squarely. "I'm sorry, but I don't know the answer to that. Benham handled all of the details with him."

I sagged back against my chair. "You can't tell me if Mr. MacGriffen is my father?"

"No," he replied, "I can't."

I put down my fork—the thought of eating any more was out of the question. I had come all this way to meet the only person who knew about my mother and father. Julian had not satisfied my curiosity about Dorie, but could anyone have done that except my mother herself? Now he was saying he didn't know who my father was. And I believed him.

Bill looked over at me, reached under the table, and patted my knee. "What *do* you know about that time?" he asked.

"I remember Doris wrote us from Boston that she was pregnant. Benham and I were working in New York and sharing an apartment. We invited Doris to come down and stay with us until the baby was born. We had a friend who knew about Spence Adoption Agency and made all the arrangements."

Now we were getting somewhere.

"Do you know if she ever saw me after I was born?" I had to ask that question that had always tormented me, even though I wasn't hopeful he would be able to answer it.

"No, I don't know that."

Another dead end. I retraced my steps. "What happened to her then?"

"She decided to stay in New York after the adoption and get a job," Julian replied more easily. "When she met Bill Horr and he asked her to marry him, she told him about having had a baby four years earlier. That didn't make any difference to Bill, and they got married in 1938. Later on they had two daughters."

"Good for Doris and for him. Can you tell me something about their daughters?" I ventured, wondering if he'd be willing to talk about my half-sisters.

"They're in their thirties now. One went to the University of Vermont and lives in California. The other went to Middlebury College and has a job in Vermont. Of course, they know nothing about you."

"Of course," I echoed dutifully. I figured I was lucky I'd been allowed to see their pictures and told as much about them as I had.

"What happened to Doris after she and Bill got married?" I asked.

"They moved out of Brooklyn eventually and settled in New Jersey. It was tough going those first years. Bill had to work hard. When things got better, they loved to play bridge, go dancing, and do social things. In later years, they took a couple of cruises to Europe."

It sounded as though my mother had had some fun in her life. That pleased me. But now I had to ask another tough question.

"When did Dorie become senile?"

I needed to know what difference it would have made if I had started looking for her sooner.

"They thought it began with a blood clot in her leg several years ago," Julian replied.

"How long ago was that?" I interrupted.

"Let's see, it must have been about three years ago, I'm not sure exactly because I was off on a trip at the time. Anyway, when the doctor operated on her, she had a stroke. I noticed she was deteriorating during this time. When I drove her into town to get her hair done, she couldn't remember the name of her hairdresser. The last time I saw her, a year and a half ago, she didn't know me at all. Bill told me this summer that she was beginning to slur her words. She used to speak quite clearly. I imagine she must be getting worse."

Listening to him describe my mother's condition, my heart sank. Now that I knew when her downward slide started, the agony of being too late rose up in me like a tidal wave. Dear God, why didn't I start looking for her in earnest sooner? Now I had to get to her before she died. Maybe, just maybe, there was still some chance that she would know me.

I couldn't think of any more questions to ask him about my mother's decline, so I shifted my focus once again.

"I'd like to get in touch with Bill Horr."

Julian seemed cautious for the first time. "Better wait. That's much closer to home."

I wondered what he meant by that. Was he afraid I wanted to see Dorie? Had he read my mind? Well, I wasn't going to get into that now.

"I plan to fly up to Vermont at the end of this weekend to look around Milton," I told him to get back on neutral ground.

"Let me draw you a map," he offered.

He pulled out his pocket-sized date book and ripped out a page. Soon he was making small sketches with his pencil.

"Here's where the general store is that my father and grandfather owned, though it's not a store any longer. It's across the street from the war memorial. Be sure to look for the name Julian Phelps on that. He's my great-uncle, whom I was named after, and he fought in the Civil War. My parents and grandparents are buried in the Milton cemetery."

He drew another little map to show where they were.

"The old family home is on this street."

Another page was filled up with a map. It was obvious he took great delight in doing this.

"It's right there at the top of the hill. We used to ski down that hill and climb back up time after time. The third floor of the house must be full of junk. It's never been cleaned out."

"You mean the house is still in your family?" I asked in surprise.

"Yes, a friend of ours who helped nurse my mother and then my father until he died is living there."

I was getting more excited as he talked. These are my roots too, I thought.

"I would also like to go out to South Hero while I'm in the area."

"There's no one living there now," Julian replied hastily. "Bill Horr left for Florida last week."

"I just want to look at the house. Do you think that would be okay?"

"I guess it's all right," he said. "Here's how to find it," he said as he ripped out another page and drew yet another map. "It's right there on Featherbed Lane."

"Featherbed Lane," I repeated, savoring the sound of it. "I love that name."

At that point, Julian looked straight at me for a moment and then said, "Maybe you do look a little like Doris. She had brown eyes, thick eyebrows, and brown hair too. Do I have brown eyes?"

I assured him he did, but all I could think about was that he saw some resemblance between my mother and me. How I craved reassurance that I looked like somebody. I guess I needed a mirror image of myself to validate my origins.

"I feel quite overwhelmed," I told Julian. "Here I am talking to a flesh-and-blood relative who is drawing me maps so I can find all the places in Vermont where the Phelpses used to live."

Julian shot right back, "Yes, and you are sitting here with a real live uncle."

I laughed, grateful that he so easily acknowledged our relationship.

"I think I have found a pretty nice uncle," I said, feeling a bit shy.

He looked over at me with a grin and said, "I think I have got a pretty nice niece."

It was all I could do to keep myself from hugging this little man who had turned out to be so engaging after our unpromising beginning over the phone.

We stayed at the roadhouse for over two hours. Try as I might, I was unable to extract any more information from Julian about Dorie. Even though she had lived with him and Benham while she was pregnant, he didn't remember any personal details about her then either. Obviously, it must have been an awkward time. I imagine that Dorie must have been feeling humiliated, grateful to her brothers for sheltering her but too ashamed to talk about her condition.

My heart ached for my mother as I pictured her carrying me in her womb those nine months. I wanted to travel back in time, put my arms around her, and reassure us both that we would be all right.

Julian seemed genuinely disappointed when we had to leave. As we were driving off, Bill said, "While you were in the restroom, Julian turned to me and asked, 'Do you know that you are married to a very remarkable person?'"

"Did he really say that?" I was elated. "I thought he was wonderful too. I've only spent a few hours with this man and yet I feel closer to him than I do to any of my aunts or uncles in my adoptive family that I've known all my life. It's probably the first time I've been truly myself with anyone outside of our own little family."

"And even though I was frustrated that Julian couldn't answer a lot of my questions, still he was so welcoming, showing me all those photos, drawing the little maps. How grateful I am to have found him."

I sat there a while, experimenting with stretching my arms and legs. Then I announced, "It may sound strange, but all of a sudden I feel there's more of me."

— 13 —

WHERE DO I BELONG?

SITTING ON THE BED with my daughter in her college dorm after our visit with Julian, I pulled the photo of my mother out of my purse to show her.

"She looks like a wonderful person," Robin said. "I'm sorry she's senile after all your work to find her."

"I know. Seeing what she looked like for the first time has made her so much more real to me. I've been wondering again what my life would have been like if she had kept me."

Reaching over to touch my hand, she replied, "I can't imagine how it would be not to know my own mom."

"You've been such a gift to me," I told her. "Having a daughter like you helped heal some of the pain and loneliness I felt growing up. I wish my adoptive mother and I could have had this kind of relationship, but the amazing thing is that my search is bringing us closer."

Later I phoned our sons, David and Frank, to catch them up on what was happening. I had told David I was searching for my birth parents when we were out visiting him in Seattle the past spring.

"What does all this have to do with me?" he had asked.

"Well," I'd responded carefully, "these are your blood relatives."

He'd changed the subject, unwilling to take the conversation further. David, like the rest of my children, loved my adoptive parents dearly. These other parents I was looking for could never take their place, nor was it my intention that they should.

This time, he was more open. When I told him my mother was senile but that I was going to try to meet her anyway, he replied, "I hope it works out for you."

When I called Frank, I told him the whole story ending by saying despairingly," I hardly know what to do at this point. It's all worked out so badly."

He listened to me calmly and then asked, "You're not going to do a one-eighty now are you, like run out and start looking for Keith James's children?"

" No," I replied, pulling myself together, "and thanks for helping me get clear. I'm just going to focus on finding my mother no matter what kind of shape she is in."

After we hung up, I couldn't help smiling as I thought of how my youngest son's matter-of-fact wisdom as well as his ability to make me laugh had lifted my spirits and helped me hone in on what really mattered.

*   *   *

After my husband returned from his meeting the next day, we drove up to Boston; from there he was flying home and I was off to Vermont.

As we waited for my plane to Burlington, Bill asked, "Are you sure you feel all right about going alone?"

"It will be good for me," I replied. "You have things you need to do back home. I want to pay attention to my own rhythm as I explore the land of my birth mother."

When my plane took off, a sense of anticipation billowed up in me. I was leaving all familiar ground and family behind to step into another reality—that of the woman who gave me life. How I had wished it would be my birth mother who was my guide. Instead it was her brother who had blessed my opening up the family secret by telling stories, showing me pictures, and drawing maps to point the way. Would this journey help me gain a greater sense of belonging in my own skin and heal all my self-doubts? Even I suspected that hope might be a bit over the top.

My feeling of belonging was disrupted the moment I learned from my adoptive parents that Leslie and I had been chosen to be their children, instead of being born in our mother's womb like our brother had been. From then on, I felt different and somehow less than. It would have been reassuring if my sister and I had been free to ask questions about where we came from. But because my past was forbidden knowledge, I could only surmise it was connected to something bad. Thus those very secrets that were supposed to protect me turned instead into a cause for shame.

I understand that my adoptive parents were following the advice of the "experts" of that era and doing the best they knew how to make Leslie and me feel part of the family. Acting as if we were their children by blood was my parents' attempt not only to keep people from judging us but also to show the world that there was no difference between all of us children in their eyes and hearts.

At the risk of being kind of obvious, not resembling anyone in my adoptive family in looks or traits was the clearest sign of my being different. I would have loved to have heard that my musical abilities came down from Aunt Mabel or that I looked exactly like my mother when I smiled. That would have helped to affirm who I was and made me feel secure knowing I had an identity that had been passed on to me through the generations of my clan.

Despite all this, I look back and have to laugh at how much my adoptive mother's way of life inspired my own choices. As a young woman, my mother worked with immigrants at Hull House in Chicago and became a friend of the founder, Jane Addams, a tireless champion for the rights of women and children. Before I was married, I too volunteered at Hull House. Later I followed my mother into politics, literally, by going to live and work with her in Washington D.C. during Adlai Stevenson's second presidential campaign. In World War II my mother volunteered with the Red Cross, working in the naval hospital nearby with wounded veterans. When we became embroiled in the Vietnam War, I volunteered at the same hospital. After our children were on their own way, we both enrolled in universities to further our education. And in our later years, we each wrote a book about our passions. These kinds of similarities make me feel grateful for the kind of woman my adoptive mother was and for all the examples of service out in the world that she provided for me.

I certainly felt I belonged in my hometown growing up. Oh my, how I loved living in that small community where I was free to ride my bike to school every day, go uptown, or over to any of my friends' homes on my own. There was a prevailing sense of safety in that outer world, which gave me stability. Best of all, I was blessed to belong to a wonderful, loyal group of girlfriends all through grade school. We were constantly getting into all sorts of mischief together as well as being a support for one another. Although they all knew I was adopted, no one ever mentioned it, probably because I didn't. What was acknowledged was that some of my friends had problems in their own families, so our home became the central meeting place because my parents graciously welcomed everyone in. We would hang out for hours in the elegant living room, laughing and gabbing, our bodies draped over the couches and chairs, Vaughan Monroe blaring love songs on the record player, while our Coca-Cola bottles made wet rings on the antique coffee table.

Would I have felt I belonged and been more secure had I lived with my birth mother in her simpler, more down-to-earth environment? Still mulling over this question, I picked up my rented car and began driving north to the town where Bill's niece and her husband lived, the couple whose wedding we had attended the past summer, and my hosts for the night.

A sign for the University of Vermont caused me to make a detour to see where my first mother had gone to college. The campus was appealing, with tall, red-brick buildings around a spacious green lawn. A group of students walked along the tree-lined sidewalk engaged in deep discussion. This was the place where my mother had studied for two years. I hoped it was a good experience for her.

The following morning I was on my way again. It had been raining all night, but soon the sun peeked through a hole in the clouds and shone down on the countryside, glorious in the late fall coloring. The hills looked as if they were covered with quilts made of bright patches of burnt orange, apple red, and butter yellow. My car window was open to welcome the crisp, fresh air. Going around a bend, Lake Champlain appeared sparkling in the morning light. Out in the middle was a large island, which must be where South Hero was, my mother's last home in Vermont. It looked inviting, but my plan was to save that final treat for tomorrow.

The road wound through a verdant valley and up a long hill, and there was Milton. Thanks to one of Julian's little maps, it was easy to find the house where my mother had spent her childhood. Parking my car out in front, I sat there staring at her home, an old Victorian three-story wood frame with a jutting dormer window in the attic. To the right was a garden that had not been cared for. The longer I stayed there, the more my body and brain began to go numb. I wasn't conscious enough then to realize I was overwhelmed by the pain of finally being here where my mother had lived, and I was too late.

Forcing myself to get out of the car and take some pictures, I tried to imagine my mother and her brothers skiing down the hill in winter. That had been about the only happy detail of her childhood Julian talked about. It would be nice to see what her home looked like inside, but how would I explain myself to the old family friend living there? Why hadn't I thought of asking my new uncle if I could introduce myself to her?

I returned to the car and made my way to the Soldiers' Monument, which consisted of a Union soldier holding a rifle against his body and standing on a marble base. "Julian Phelps" was engraved on the bottom with all the rest. This was my great-great-uncle who had served in the Civil War, a part of my history that should make me feel proud, but I was unable to muster up any emotion at all. The general store was supposed to be just across the street, but the only building I saw was one that said LAUNDROMAT above it. I went over to look anyway, and there engraved in the stone step leading up to the door I spied the name, O. G. PHELPS & SON. So this had been the store after all.

I walked up the hill to where three red brick buildings stood and discovered that one of them was the Town Hall. Maybe the town clerk could tell me about the Phelps family. Just as I was opening the door, reality hit. What right did the illegitimate daughter have going around asking leading questions? In a small town like this, anything a stranger said would be noticed. Who knows, the town clerk could even have been one of Dorie's daughters. I turned away. Although Julian had accepted me wholeheartedly as his niece, he had made it clear I was not to tell my half-sisters of my existence.

It was becoming obvious as well that I didn't belong in my mother's hometown. Would I have fit in here as a child with my unmarried mother, who would in all probability have been living with her parents, raising her daughter? In today's world where it's acceptable for an unwed woman to keep her child, that might have worked, but back then? I already knew the answer to that question and knew that wasn't the life I would have wanted to live.

A public telephone was on the wall of the Town Hall. I called the airlines and changed my reservation from tomorrow to later that afternoon. There seemed to be no point in prolonging my Vermont visit longer than necessary.

Now all there was left to see in Milton was the cemetery. I didn't have to worry about causing talk there. Dead people wouldn't mind my curiosity or care who I was. Clutching another of the invaluable maps, I climbed the hill and found O. G. Phelps's large stone monument. Nearby were the graves of Dorie's parents: Ethel Benham Phelps (1876–1947) and Karl G. Phelps (1873–1955). As I gazed down at those names, the fog that had enveloped me ever since being at my mother's home receded. I was here at the final resting place of my grandparents, claiming my ancestry. Never again would I lament over not having a past or knowing about my roots. These rough stone slabs standing guard over my grandparents' remains grounded me to the earth in a way that nothing else could do.

Feeling renewed, I drove back to the highway and soon came to the causeway over Lake Champlain that connected the mainland to the island. A sign saying "South Hero" greeted me. Almost immediately Featherbed Lane appeared on the right. I made myself keep going toward the town because I wanted to save Dorie's home for the last. As it turned out, South Hero was so tiny that I drove right through it before realizing that the few little stores—two funky-looking eateries and the town clerk's office—were it. Turning around and starting back, a sign saying "Apples Here" on the side of a red barn caught my eye. I went in, remembering I'd not had any lunch, and bought three beautiful red ones. The shopkeeper smiled and wished me a pleasant day out on the island.

Buoyed by her kindness and revived by eating one of the crunchy, tart apples, I felt ready to see my mother's final home in Vermont. At least this time I had Julian's permission to look around. When I turned into the driveway off Featherbed Lane, I saw that both the garage in front and the house down the hill behind it were built of large, round logs painted a distinctive shade of green. I got out and walked over to her home, a simple two-story set back about fifty feet from the bluff above Lake Champlain. It was hard to see in the windows, which were too high, but there was a large glassed-in porch in back, which must have afforded a perfect view of the lake.

A wooden deck about eight-by-fifteen feet standing out on the edge of the bluff caught my attention. Next to it was a towering maple tree resplendent in a cloak of golden leaves, which shimmered in the afternoon sun. I went over and stepped up on the platform. Below stretched the shoreline, where I could look in both directions for miles and see no other dwelling. The water, a deep sapphire blue, was rippling in the breeze. A gust rose up the hill and playfully swirled around my body.

I pictured my mother sitting out here, and then I saw myself sitting next to her, both of us enjoying the peace and beauty. I felt myself taking her hand and acknowledging how hard it must have been to have given birth to me and then go through the pain of giving me up because there was no other choice for either of us back then. I let her know that my life has been a good one. I told her how much I admired her for possessing the courage and integrity to be honest with Bill Horr about me, knowing she was risking her future happiness, and that I was glad she picked the kind of man who would love her anyway. I said how happy I was that she gave birth to two more daughters, ones she could raise with pride and joy. And how fitting that she came to live in this sublime place and find contentment. By now, tears of love and gratitude were running down my cheeks.

A faint sound began emanating from out of nowhere, like softly falling rain—only it wasn't raining. Instead what looked like snowflakes began fluttering down upon me, but it was too warm for snow. I held out my hand and caught one as it floated by. It was hard like hail but flat instead of round. When I tasted it, the coolness lingered on my tongue. Looking about for the source of this manna, I saw it coming from above my head, but it fell only on the platform, neither on the surrounding ground nor into the lake below. Time and space lost all meaning as I stood there marveling in the mystery of those delicate white petals dancing around my body.

When I finally stepped off the platform, the precipitation stopped as abruptly as it had begun. Was it some aberration in the weather pattern, a kind of sign, or perhaps a benediction from heaven? All of these were possible, but in my heart of hearts I knew it was my precious mother thanking me for understanding why she had to let me go by sending me her own sweet blessing. As I walked back to the car, a healing balm was flowing through my being, and I knew that no matter what happened, in the end all would be well.

— *14* —

WE MEET

WHEN I CAME HOME from Vermont, all my thoughts and energy were focused on my birth mother. I had to get to her as quickly as possible. Time was running out. That meant calling Bill Horr, even if I squandered Julian's good will by ignoring his request to hold back. After getting Bill's number in Florida from Information, I wrote out two different speeches, preparing myself for whether he proved difficult or welcoming. Asking God to be with me, I braced myself and dialed.

The same cheery voice that I had spoken to in Vermont answered. "Bill Horr here."

"Hi, this is Titia Ellis," I began, trying to keep my voice from trembling. "I talked to you a while ago when I was looking for my mother's uncles. I couldn't tell you who I really was back then because I didn't know if you knew of my existence."

"Yes, I knew," he interrupted.

My heart stopped. What did he just say? I hadn't even told him who I was yet. "Have you been talking to Julian?"

"No," he replied quickly.

My hand was so clammy that I could hardly hold onto the phone. What was happening here? I had been all geared up to make my case to this man, and he didn't seem to need it in the least.

"Oh," I said, recovering my ability to speak. "My husband and I had a wonderful lunch with Julian last week. Then I flew up to Vermont where, thanks to his help, I saw the family home, the one in South Hero, and much more. It was very meaningful for me."

"I'm sure it was," he replied kindly.

"But now I would like to meet you and talk about Dorie. I'm broken-hearted that she's senile."

"Yes, it's tragic. She's had so many awful problems these last several years. She's just a tired little old lady who doesn't have much going for her. She doesn't even know me or the girls anymore."

I felt sick hearing him say that, but I wasn't going to give up on my plan to meet my mother. I was her firstborn. Julian had even said I looked like her. That had meant a great deal to me.

He added as if reading my mind, "I won't take you to see her. I don't take anyone to see her these days."

I contracted as if I had just been punched in the stomach. Not see my mother? After all I had been through to get to this point? How could he decide that? I wanted to shout: *I must see my mother! It's my right!* But thank goodness, that inner voice told me to slow down and say nothing. I could work on him when I got down to Florida.

"That must be very hard on you," was all I replied.

"I've come to accept it. She almost died a few years back. What more can I tell you?"

Taking a big breath, I said, "Instead of discussing this on the phone, I would much rather come down to Florida and talk to you in person, if that's okay with you. You knew her better than anyone. There's a lot I would like to know."

"Sure," Bill responded easily. "When would you like to come?"

"As soon as possible," I was emboldened by his kindness. "What are you doing this weekend?"

"Well, Friday I have to go to Fort Lauderdale. Saturday, I'm playing bridge. I'm sorry about that. I would have taken you to dinner Saturday night."

Undaunted, I asked, "How about Sunday or Monday?"

"That would be fine. I'm not doing anything then."

"Let's see, I have clients all day Monday so I'd better come Sunday. I'll probably get down Saturday afternoon and call when I get in." Suddenly aware I had no idea where Venice, Florida, was, I asked, "What airport do I fly into?"

"Sarasota would be the nearest."

"Great. I'll be seeing you soon, and thanks so much, Bill. I appreciate your being willing to let me come on such short notice."

I hung up the phone and sank down on the bed. What a friendly, welcoming man who seemed totally unfazed by this desperate woman wanting to see him ASAP. Although neither of us had actually acknowledged that Dorie was my mother, he appeared to be aware of just who I was. He must have talked to Julian. There was no other way he could have known.

While I was at it, why not make the most of my time and go to Florida for the whole weekend? When I was a teenager, our family often went down to Boca Grande during spring vacation and rented a cottage. I had loved it there. Maybe I would drive over and see what it looked like thirty years later. Picking up the phone, I called the airlines and made my reservation.

Bill was finishing up his breakfast when I walked in and announced, "I just talked to Bill Horr. He already knew about me and couldn't have been nicer. I'm going down to see him and find my mother this Friday."

My husband almost choked on his cereal. "You're going down to Florida to see this man in two days? But you said you'd go duck hunting with me this weekend."

"Oh, dear, I'm sorry. I forgot all about that."

"You have to come! All the other wives will be there."

By this time, he was almost shouting.

"Honey, I just can't do it. Everybody will be shooting those poor birds, and you know how much I hate that. This weekend I have to go find my mother. I can't stop now."

"I don't believe I'm hearing this," he said, his face bright red, as he hurried from the room.

I started to go after him to try to make everything all right, but I stopped myself. *Wait. Talk to him when he has calmed down.* To work off my own energy, I called to Cola and headed out to the lake. On the way, I agonized over what a strain my search had caused in our marriage. I felt torn in two. I had to find my birth mother, but I loved this man, and I could be in serious danger of losing him in the process.

That night as we lay far apart in bed, I said, "I'm sorry I forgot about the hunting weekend. Guess I'm pretty tuned into my own journey right now."

"You sure are," he fumed. "I feel as if I don't count with you anymore. I go with you to see John MacGriffen and Julian. You don't come hunting with me or do much of anything else that matters to me these days."

His words hit home. "You're right. You have been such a support to me during all this, and I have done so little—well nothing really—for you. Can you hold on just a bit longer? I know this hasn't been easy for you."

"Well, it helps to have you acknowledge that. Promise me this won't go on much more. I don't think I can take it."

"I just have to see my mother. Then I'll be done."

Little did either of us know then that was a promise I could not keep.

I reached out and found his hand in the dark. "Hang in there with me. I need you."

He squeezed my hand in return. "Well, I need you too, and I've been having trouble finding you."

"I know. I'm totally driven, but I have to keep going."

"I guess you do," he sighed. "So when do I take you to the airport?"

I laughed from relief and gratefulness. "Thanks. You're the best."

*   *   *

"Are you going to be okay doing this?" Bill asked as we drove to O'Hare on Friday. "It could be a pretty tough visit."

"I have to do this final piece. I'm afraid with every passing day that my chances of connecting with my mother are lessening. And I'm scared I'll get all the way down there, and Bill Horr won't let me meet her. But if that happens, I've decided I'll go through the Yellow Pages and phone every nursing home in the area. I'll stay until I find her, cancel all my clients for the next week if I have to."

"If anyone could do it, it would be you," he said.

"Thanks for understanding," I said after we had kissed good-bye. "This will all be over soon."

"I hope you're right," he said fervently.

When I took my seat on the plane, I noticed that the crew members were wearing masks or black hats. What was going on? Then I realized it was Halloween. The passengers were all laughing and taking pictures. How ironic that I was going to find my mother on this holiday. She would be wearing the mask of senility. *Oh, God, please help me reach through it to who she is inside.*

Arriving in Sarasota in the early afternoon, I picked up my rental car, consulted the map, and discovered that Boca Grande was only about fifty miles down the coast. After checking into a motel upon my arrival, I changed into my bathing suit, went over to the beach, and jumped into the ocean. It felt like heaven being in the warm salt water. For over an hour, I frolicked in the waves, lay on the hot sand, and looked for shells. I became that young girl again who had been so happy and free in this place. The next morning, I took a long walk along the beach. Bending down to pick up an especially beautiful conch shell, I suddenly had this knowing that one day I would write the story of my search. Excitement began pumping through me.

Driving through Fort Myers on my way to Venice, I spotted a sign for Thomas Edison's home and museum. On the spur of the moment, I decided to go see it. My adoptive grandfather had collaborated with Edison to invent an office machine—the source of the family fortune—and in the process they had become friends. As I wandered through the museum, I thought about how my father's wealth had allowed me a life of great privilege. At that moment, I experienced the full impact of my good fortune to be adopted into a family who had opened up so much of the world for me. As that awareness settled in, a wave of gratitude washed over me.

Later, I called Bill Horr from a pay phone to find out the plans for our meeting the next day.

"I want to take you out for lunch," he said. "How much time do you have tomorrow before you're flying back?"

"I'll be there for the whole day," I replied. He didn't need to know that I was planning on staying until I had seen my mother, no matter how long that might take.

"How about coming to my house around ten thirty in the morning?"

That night in a motel just outside of Venice, I sat for a long time over dinner, reflecting on all that had happened. Coming down early to Florida had been a good change of pace for me. I had been moving so fast these last few weeks that I had needed a respite to prepare myself for this all-too-crucial meeting with my mother.

I understand now that on some unconscious level, I knew that being with her was not going to work out the way I had hoped. To cope with that, I had propped myself up with good memories of my life with my adoptive family.

Taking time out had also resulted in the discovery that I would some day write about my search. Although I didn't know it then, the work of writing would require my own unmasking, lead me to my own wisdom, and in the end, create a deeper connection to myself than I had ever dreamed possible.

Later that evening, I started checking out nursing homes in the phone directory. When I had written down the first ten with their phone numbers and addresses, I stopped. The listings for nursing homes took up two whole pages. To call every one of them, I would have to stay longer than two days. Obviously, Florida's west coast was a mecca for storing the sick and aged. How would I ever find where my mother was with this many options available?

Arriving at Bill's home the next morning, I felt my heart beating wildly. I rang the bell of his small, one-story, gray wood home, which had a front porch with two green aluminum chairs on it and a minute plot of grass to the side.

"Hello, Titia," Bill said, smiling broadly, as he opened the door.

I gazed at the man who carried my hopes in his hands. He was short like Julian—only a few inches taller than I—his gray hair crew cut, thick gray eyebrows, and glasses. His body looked fit as if he did a daily workout.

"Welcome to my modest villa."

The inside of the house was simple, a couch and two chairs in the living room area with a small kitchen to one side. Just in front was a square, brown wood table, where two blue cotton table mats were set out. Bill brought in a plate of sugared doughnuts from the kitchen and put it on the table.

"Please sit down," he said as he gestured to one of the chairs. "How do you like your coffee?"

"Black would be fine, thanks."

"So how was your trip?" he asked, pouring the coffee.

We made small talk for the next several minutes. Suddenly he stopped and looked me straight in the eye.

"I know you didn't come here to talk to me. I imagine you would like to go and see your mother."

My whole body began to shake. Tears pricked my eyes.

"I would like that very much," I managed to say.

"I've made arrangements for us to go see her in about an hour," he said matter-of-factly.

"How kind of you." I could hardly believe this was happening. He was making it easy for me, just as he had done in our phone conversation when I had asked to come see him. And he had said "your mother" so naturally. He had acknowledged who I was.

"Would you like to hear how her illness came on?" Bill asked.

When I said yes, he proceeded to recite much the same story that Julian had told me and then added, "My minister told me about a woman who took people into her home to care for them. I invited her over to meet us, and we both liked her. I agonized about turning Doris over to someone else's care, but I just couldn't do it any longer."

He looked at me, his eyes pleading for understanding.

"It must have been very difficult for you," I said.

"Last summer, I arranged for the nurse to bring Doris up to South Hero for five days. She'd always loved it up there. But she didn't even know where she was. It was sad."

Again, he looked over at me helplessly.

"I admire you for how hard you've tried," I sympathized.

"Thank you." Bill looked relieved. It was as if he were seeking my approval, as Doris's oldest daughter, for his actions.

"I really have done my best. I go over and see her every other day when I'm down here. She has no idea who I am, but I think she realizes I'm someone special."

My heart sank hearing those words. I was going back and forth between hope and despair. I wanted to hold on to the dream that my mother would know me, but I was being forced to face the reality that she knew no one anymore.

Bill said that it was time to go. My stomach was so tied up in knots driving over that I hardly heard a word he was saying. I was going to see my mother whom I had lost forty-six years ago. What would she be like? Would she remember me?

Give me strength to handle this, I prayed silently.

We pulled up in front of a blue bungalow on a small side street. *So much for finding my mother on my own,* I thought.

"Here we are," Bill announced.

I walked on shaking legs up to the front door, which was opened immediately by a tall, thin woman, about forty, with long blond hair in a braid down her back.

"Hi, Sara. This is Mrs. Ellis, a close friend of the family."

"Please come in. Doris is waiting for you." She led us down the hall and into a small white room with blue curtains at the window. My quick glance took in the bed—empty, neatly made up. Then I saw her, a tiny, withered old woman dwarfed by the big chair in which she sat, her legs propped up on an ottoman. Her short gray hair was brushed back from her deeply lined face, which caused her dark eyes and thick eyebrows to stand out. She was wearing a pink and white striped shirt, white slacks, and sandals.

"This is Mrs. Ellis," Bill said.

Her face turned toward me. I stared into a pair of vacant brown eyes.

Bill gently nudged me into a straight-backed chair opposite my mother. Then he sat down next to me. Sara stood by the door.

"It's good to see you," I managed to croak, my mouth so dry I could barely speak.

This was my mother. I had finally found her. Whenever I'd imagined this moment, I thought I would be ecstatic. Now my mother was sitting three feet away from me, and she was old in body and spirit, broken in mind. I looked at her closely, searching desperately for some resemblance between us. There was nothing. Finally I saw her fingernails, flat, blunt, different from the norm. I had those same nails, as did my daughter. So there it was—our only similarity came down to this.

"How are you feeling today?" Bill asked her.

She looked at him and opened her mouth to reply, "I, uh, I ..." Nothing more came forth. She had drifted off into the white night of her empty mind.

I was here with my mother, but she wasn't present. She just sat immobilized, looking blankly from one person to another.

A little black and white dog ran into the room. My mother seemed to wake up. She watched it intently, a ghost of a smile flitting across her face. Reaching down, she tried to pat it, but the dog turned and darted out of the room before she could touch it.

"Mrs. Ellis was up in South Hero," Bill said.

She looked at him, aware that something was expected of her. Then she laughed, a disembodied sound, eerie and inappropriate. A cold shiver ran through me.

Bill and Sara talked about her bringing Doris up to South Hero last summer.

"You were really cold," Bill teased her. "I think you were wearing two jackets by the time we got to the house."

Sara laughed. Dorie laughed too, that awful laugh, far more upsetting than fingernails dragging across a blackboard because this unearthly noise was coming from my mother.

Although I had been to South Hero and knew where they were taking about, it didn't matter. All I wanted was to connect with the woman who bore me. Instead I was being introduced to my own mother as "Mrs. Ellis" and trapped in the room with her two guardians. This visit was a charade. We were all dressed up in our nice clothes, wearing our smiley masks, pretending to be cheery. It was a nightmare, far worse than any Halloween scenario.

I have agonized since over why I couldn't break through to my mother when it mattered so much to me. Why did I not ask the other two to leave the room so that I could talk to her alone? Even if it did not result in her recognizing me, at least I would have done everything I could to make contact. After achieving my goal at long last, why did I lose all my hard-won strength and determination and sit in that room paralyzed, just like my mother? All I can think of is that finally seeing my mother and facing the bitter reality of her senility was more than I could handle. I became as helpless as a newborn babe. Added to that, being the good daughter that I was, I felt indebted to her husband, who had made this visit possible. God forbid that I do something that might upset him, or her, or anyone else.

Instead I did all that I was capable of in that moment. I poured out my heart silently to my mother.

Mommy, I've come back to you. I finally found you after all these years. Thank you for bearing me. I love you. I've always known you were a beautiful person, inside as well as out. I wanted you to hold me and love me, but I understand why you had to give me up. Don't worry; you made the only choice you could. I'm glad to be here with you.

But there my focus failed. It was not true. I was not glad; I was in anguish. I had found my mother, but she was no longer there. I was too late. My mother's unnerving laugh at something Sara just said intensified my loss.

Oh, please don't feel you have to do that, I begged silently.

It would take me years before I understood that her laughter was the only way left for my mother to be cheerful and a part of the conversation going on around her. She was just doing the best she was able to join in.

Bill stood up. He bent over and kissed his wife on the cheek. She didn't move or react in any way. I sat there feeling as dead as my mother, all the life force drained out of me.

I looked at her and thought, *I just found you and now I have to leave you. And you don't even know who I am. I can't speak aloud the words that are on my heart. And would I be able to reach you, had I been free to do those things?*

Bill cleared his throat, signaling that it was time to leave. I managed to pull myself up from the chair and say woodenly, "It was good to see you"—the very words I had spoken when I walked in and was introduced to my birth mother for the first and last time.

Walking unsteadily out of the room, I bumped into the doorway.

In the hallway, Sara looked at me quizzically. "Are you a relative of Doris's?"

"Yes," I responded lifelessly. "I am."

— 15 —

ALL IS NOT LOST

I HAD FOUND MY mother, but it was too late. The despair that engulfed me turned into numbness. Bill Horr was kind, took me to lunch, and questioned me about how I found them. Talking about my search helped me come alive again, especially since he was such a good listener. But when I got to the John MacGriffen part and asked if my mother ever told Bill who my father was, he knew nothing. My last hope of finding that answer vanished.

When we came back to his home, I felt strong enough to ask more about the kind of person my mother was. Bill was happy to oblige. I learned that she was a good housekeeper, a cheerful person, and a loyal friend.

"We really struggled in the early part of our marriage," he continued. "My business caused me to live away from home during the week for several years. Doris raised our daughters all by herself. It must have been hard for her, but she never complained. That shows you the kind of person she was."

"I admire her for that," I said, genuinely moved. "I can't imagine raising my children on my own."

I asked him when they had moved to South Hero.

"That came later when I retired and we had more money. It was hard to make friends there at first. I did odd jobs for people and helped raise money for our church's renovation. Doris was constantly at the church, working in the ladies' groups. After a while, we were accepted."

"Did she like it up there?"

"Oh, yes, it was good for both of us. A few years later, we started taking trips in the winter. We both loved to travel. We enjoyed going dancing too."

I smiled, pleased to hear that my mother had these good times before the last years of illness.

Bill returned my smile. "If you ever get to Vermont again, I certainly hope you and your hubby will come see me in South Hero. I could show you all the old photographs I have up there."

"Thank you," I said gratefully. "We'd love to visit you."

I asked how he knew who I was when I called him the second time.

"You must have talked to Julian."

Bill laughed, "You're right. I stopped on my way down to Florida to visit Julian. You and your husband had just been there the day before. When he showed me the photo you sent of your family all standing outside the Middlebury Chapel, I couldn't believe it. I'm a Middlebury graduate myself and a fervent supporter of the place."

"What a wonderful set of coincidences," I said happily, "or was that just all part of a larger plan?"

Later in the day, each of his daughters phoned. I went out on the porch in order not to intrude, but I couldn't help hearing everything he said. It seemed surreal. He was talking to my half-sisters, Lois and Susan. What would they say if they knew who was with him?

"You sound like you have a very close relationship with both of them," I told him when he came out to join me, and then I felt impelled to say, "Do you realize they are my half-sisters?"

"Yes," he nodded, smiling, "and I would add that you are my third daughter."

I was so touched he would say such a thing that I said, "You are just the kind of stepfather I would love to have."

But then his expression became serious. "Of course, the girls don't know anything about you. I would like to keep it that way. It could upset them and ruin their relationship with their mother if they knew what she had done."

It was as if all the air had just been let out of me. This man had been so welcoming, inviting me to visit him, even calling me his third daughter. Why couldn't I tell my sisters? We had all shared the same womb. It seemed crazy to think that would stop them from loving their mother. Keeping this a secret didn't seem fair to me or to them either.

But I owed Bill Horr a lot, so I simply said, "I understand. I won't say anything."

Even as I promised that, I was already nursing the hope that maybe someday I would meet both Susan and Lois. I wouldn't have to tell them who I was. I would be content to be just some distant relative. Little did I know how soon I would be put to the test.

*   *   *

Back at home, I tried to concentrate more on my husband when I wasn't coping with my despair over my mother. I wrote Bill Horr, thanking him for everything and asked that he keep me updated on my mother's condition. Several months later he replied saying Doris was now totally bedridden and that he was hoping we would visit him in the summer up in South Hero. I wrote back saying fall would be better after we'd recovered from our daughter's wedding. In May, I sent him a present to give Dorie for Mother's Day, a pair of soft white cotton pajamas decorated with tiny sprigs of pink flowers. Somehow that small act helped ease a fraction of my pain over being unable to reach through to my mother at our only meeting since she gave me life.

At the end of August, I called Bill and arranged for us to drop by and pay him a short visit when we toured around Vermont in the middle of September. As the time grew close, I was looking forward to being with him again and seeing photos of my mother as well as showing my husband my ancestral roots.

*   *   *

It was September 10, always a special day because David, our first child, arrived shortly after midnight on this date twenty-three years ago. I was getting dressed, eager for the time to go by, so I could call him in Seattle. Just then, the phone rang. Wondering who would be telephoning at this hour, I answered.

A familiar voice said, "Bill Horr here. Is this Titia?"

"Yes. Hi, Bill, how are you?" I asked, assuming he was calling to make final plans for our visit.

"I have some bad news." His voice was shaky. "I received a call from Florida a few hours ago that Doris died during the night."

"Oh, no." I felt as if all the blood had just drained out of my heart.

"She apparently had a massive stroke and died in her bed. There was no suffering. You saw how she was last fall. It's been downhill ever since."

"Yes, I remember." I could barely speak.

"I'll be leaving for Florida tomorrow. I'm sorry we won't be able to get together in Vermont next week after all."

"Of course. I understand."

"I'll have a memorial service in South Hero for her," Bill continued, sounding stronger as he talked about plans. "Then there will be another one for her in Venice when her friends come back down for the winter. I'll let you know when those are."

I finally found my voice. "Thank you, Bill, for calling. I'm so sorry for you and the girls."

We hung up. I sank down on our unmade bed, holding my head in my hands.

"She's gone. My mother is gone. I've lost her."

I began rocking back and forth. I couldn't even cry. Finally I flung myself face down on the bed, and pulled the covers over me. I wanted to drown out everything. I don't know how long I had been there when an inner voice broke through my anguish.

You found her. You listened to that warning that she would be dead within the year. If you hadn't stopped working on your dissertation and focused all your attention on searching for her, you would never have seen her. Then you'd never forgive yourself.

It was true, I thought. I had done that. Acknowledging this gave me the strength to pull myself together and go downstairs to seek comfort from Bill.

He was sitting at the breakfast table reading the paper. "Who was that on the phone earlier?"

"It was Bill Horr," I said woodenly, "calling to tell me that my mother had just died."

He stood up and came over to me. "Oh, how terribly sad for you."

I stepped into his outstretched arms. The tears that had been blocked began to run down my face.

"I'll never see my mother again," I sobbed against his chest. "It's over. And now we can't go to Vermont next week and visit him. I should have pushed myself to go see him in August no matter how tired I was after the wedding. I blew it."

He held me close as I poured out my pain.

At last, wrung out, the tears stopped flowing.

"Thank God, I have you," I said, wiping my eyes.

"Do you feel like some breakfast?" Bill asked.

"I couldn't eat a thing right now. I think I'll take the dog and get some air."

I walked along the road toward the lake, Cola staying close by my side as if sensing my need for her. Each step pounded in the bitter truth. My mother was dead. I never had a chance to know her. My heart felt heavy, sodden with grief. It was comforting to step into the silent embrace of the tall pines guarding the path down from the bluff. When we arrived at the beach, I automatically picked up a stick and threw it into the water. Cola jumped in, swam out to fetch it, and then returned, tail wagging, eager for more.

"Not now," I said, patting her sleek wet fur.

I stood on the sand staring out at the vast expanse of Lake Michigan. It was a clear day. The water was calm and serene. Spying an old log at the edge of the beach, I sat down on it, took off my sandals, and dangled my feet in the cool liquid.

The gentle rippling of the waves was mesmerizing. Coming in, going out. Coming in, going out. The dance resonated within my body. I moved into a different reality. This was the eternal rhythm, and I was being bathed in a great watery womb. A seagull flew overhead, shrieking. That was part of the dance too. The sun shone across the water, creating a golden path that floated toward my feet. In that instant, I knew that my mother was with me. Her presence was all around me, her love washing me clean. I sat there a long time, tears falling down my cheeks, but they were no longer tears of sadness. I was crying for joy because now I understood that even though we had been separated physically throughout my lifetime, the connection between us had never been broken on the spiritual plane. Nor had it ended with her passing. The fact that my mother had died on the very same date that I had produced my first biological child was no coincidence either. To me it was just another sign that her soul had been watching over me always and that she would continue to do so until we met on the other side.

The heat from the sun on my face finally roused me. I rose unsteadily, stretched out my arms, and silently thanked my mother for blessing me once again. Cola came over and nuzzled my leg while I put on my sandals. Together we made our way back up the path. When we returned home, Bill rushed out the back door. "Where were you? You've been gone so long I was getting worried."

He stopped and looked at me more closely. "What's happened to you? You look different, so radiant."

"I was at the lake. It was wonderful. I met my mother there."

"I don't know what you mean by that," he responded, "but something's sure changed in you."

"And walking home," I said, "I had this most amazing idea."

"Oh, no," he groaned. "What now?"

"Well, we have this trip to New England all arranged for next week. Let's still do it. We'll go to Vermont for the first three days, just the way we were planning, and tour around."

My excitement grew as the words spilled out of me.

"And just maybe while we're there, my mother's memorial service will take place in South Hero. I guess that sounds crazy, but who knows? Anything is possible. Think what it would be like if I could be there for that. I'd also have the chance to meet my two half-sisters and see Bill Horr and Julian again."

"It's such a long shot," my husband protested. "Your mother just died. Bill Horr told you he was going down to Florida. There can't be a service next week in South Hero. He could never pull it off that quickly. And even if we did come on the right date, would he want you there? Remember he said that his daughters were never to know about you."

"They wouldn't have to know the truth. I could pass myself off as some distant relative traveling through town who'd heard about the funeral and wanted to pay my respects."

"I can tell that your mind is made up," Bill said in a resigned tone.

"Okay, we'll go to Vermont after all, but please don't get your hopes up too much. I'd hate to see you crushed again."

"I'll be all right."

I thought back to my time at the lake, still feeling her love around me.

"I believe my mother wants me to be there."

— 16 —

SPIRITUAL CONNECTION

FLYING TO VERMONT THE next Wednesday, I was holding on to the hope that I was going to attend my birth mother's memorial service. Despite his promise, Bill Horr had never phoned to tell me when the service was to be held. Yet all during the week since my mother died, I became more convinced that my mother wanted me there. It wasn't as if I heard her voice telling me to come. I just knew intuitively that she was guiding me. If I couldn't be with her in life, at least I could be present to honor her in death.

My husband was less optimistic.

"I still think you're nuts to expect the service to be taking place this soon," he said as we landed in Burlington. "How will you find out anyway? Surely you're planning to call Bill Horr and at least see if he's back in Vermont?"

"Not now. I'm just taking this one step at a time."

I knew his urging me to make that phone call was entirely reasonable, but I wasn't going to be pushed. There was no way to explain to this man I lived with, who had been trained all his life to be logical, that I was following a kind of knowing not based on facts.

"All I can tell you is that Bill said there was going to be a service in South Hero."

"But he's probably still down in Florida."

"He said he was going down there, but he might have been able to make all the arrangements by now. Don't worry; I'll call him when the time is right. My only concern is what to do if one of my half-sisters is at the house and answers the phone. Who will I say I am? I didn't handle that well with Darcy MacGriffen. This time I can't afford to make any mistakes. I've promised their father I won't tell them about me."

"Make it brief and vague. Just say you're a distant cousin," he advised. "You always feel you have to give too many explanations."

Touché. My husband may not have understood my reasons for going, but he was right on target about me there.

We picked up our rental car and, at my suggestion, drove out to South Hero. Somehow I knew my mother's final home in Vermont should be our first destination. Bill was not as certain.

"I think we're taking a big chance coming here," he said anxiously. "You don't want to blow everything by walking in on all your family uninvited, if indeed they are gathered for the service."

"You're right," I agreed. "That would be terrible. We'll just look around first and see if anyone's there."

We arrived at the house and cautiously drove in the driveway. Not a car was in sight.

"It seems safe. Let's get out," I said eagerly.

"Someone could be out in back," Bill warned.

"There doesn't seem to be a sign of life. Come on," I begged, "I want you to see the platform where I had that remarkable experience with my mother."

I'll admit it does look like I took an enormous risk by going to my mother's home. If I ran into one of the family, it could have destroyed the very thing I wanted—to be deemed trustworthy enough to be invited to her service. Yet despite the stakes being so high, I never worried about being discovered.

Reluctantly, Bill followed me around to the deck overlooking Lake Champlain. We stood for a while on the platform holding hands and gazing out at the water below. *I'm here,* I said silently to my mother. When we walked back to the house, I felt compelled to climb up on a ledge and peer in a window. Bill was horrified. But there in the living room on the coffee table lay just the clue I needed—a membership book for the United Church of South Hero.

"Their church! That's where we need to go!" I shouted, so excited that I almost fell in my haste to scramble down from my perch. "They'll be able to tell us when the service is."

We drove at a rapid pace through town and found the church off on a side road. I jumped out of the car, bounded up the steps to the entrance, and almost bumped into a man who opened the door in my face.

"Good day," he said pleasantly. "You seem like you're in a hurry. Are you looking for someone?"

"Yes," I said breathlessly, "we're from out of state and we're friends of Doris Horr's. We heard there was going to be a memorial service for her and wondered when it might be."

"Well, you've come to the right person. I'm the interim pastor, and I think her service is coming up. Let's see, the church bulletin will tell us the exact date."

He picked up one lying on the table by the door and opened it. My body was so tense that I could hardly move my feet over to see where he was pointing.

"Here it is." He began to read from the bulletin. "Memorial service for Doris Phelps Horr at eleven o'clock on Saturday, the eighteenth of September."

He thought for a moment and then said, "Yes, that's this Saturday."

Letting out my breath with an audible sigh, I said, "Thank you."

"Good, you can be here for it," beamed the minister. "Now, let me show you around. The church was rebuilt a while ago after it was struck by lightning."

I did my best to admire the results. It was a lovely simple space, painted sky blue, light and airy with tall glass windows. I remembered Bill Horr telling me how he had helped raise the money for its reconstruction and that my mother had faithfully attended all the women's groups here.

The minister kept talking. I kept nodding, scarcely hearing a word. Bill finally came in to see what was taking me so long.

"Here's my husband. Sorry, we have to run now. Thanks so much."

I was out the door before the minister could finish his sentence.

"My mother's service is this Saturday," I announced excitedly as we got back into our car. "What do you think of that?"

He shook his head. "It's incredible. You are one lucky lady."

"It's not luck," I told him, suddenly dead serious. "It's what my mother wanted for me. I've been thinking a lot about this. My only meeting with her down in Florida was disastrous because her mind and body had declined so badly. But the two times I've communicated with her spirit—once before she died and then down at the lake afterward—even though I couldn't see or touch her, her presence was as real to me as anything I've ever felt.

"After all," I concluded, "I did spend nine months forming in her womb, soaking up her genes, her blood, her nurturing love. And now she is guiding me."

Poor Bill could only shake his head.

"Whatever makes sense to you is what counts."

I smiled at him. "Thanks for saying that instead of threatening to have me locked up."

"But the part I can't get over," he continued, shaking his head, "is that your mother's service is actually happening in three days, and we are here. Now what do we do until then?"

"Let's just go sightseeing as we had planned, but change our plane reservation on Saturday from the morning to the afternoon. We'll start by going over to Milton so I can show you all the family sites."

Later, standing outside my mother's childhood home, I turned to him. "What a difference it makes coming back here with you after all that has happened. I no longer feel as if I were just the illegitimate daughter sneaking into town. Instead, I'm a woman who is fortunate enough to have two exceptional families, and I'm showing my husband where my birth clan came from."

We spent that night with Bill's niece and her family. They couldn't wait to show me a notice about my mother's memorial service in the local newspaper.

"That's why we're here," I said. "I've been incredibly driven in this search, but I'm coming down the home stretch. My mother's memorial service is the final piece."

I felt an unexpected pang as I spoke. Was that really going to be the end of everything? What about my half-sisters?

At our bed and breakfast on Friday morning, I worked up my nerve to talk to my mother's husband. My Bill had gone out to buy a paper, understanding that I needed to be alone when I made this crucial call.

Clutching the phone, I said a quick prayer to my mother's spirit:

Please tell Bill Horr to let me come to your service. Then I dialed the number in South Hero.

It was a relief to hear him answer. At least I wouldn't have to deal with explaining who I was to my half-sisters.

"Hi, Bill. This is Titia. How are you doing?" I began, trying to ignore the huge knot in my stomach.

"Oh, I've been pretty busy. I flew down to Florida right after I got the news. That was tough." His voice cracked. Pulling himself together, he continued, "I just got back here yesterday. We're having a little memorial service for her in South Hero tomorrow."

My heart warmed to him. It wasn't the time to tell him I was here nor did it matter that he hadn't called to let me know about the service. My mother had taken care of all that.

"This must be painful for you."

"Yes," he responded heavily, "it is. Of course, I've known for the past year and a half that she could die anytime. But now that it's final, I feel pretty hard hit."

"I'm sorry," I said softly.

"You never came to Vermont?" he asked, shifting gears.

I took a deep breath. "Actually, my husband and I are here right now. We had already made all our reservations, so we decided just to come ahead. We've been visiting Bill's niece and her family in Chelsea."

Here goes, I thought, taking a deep breath. "Bill, I would very much like to come to my mother's service tomorrow. Would that be all right with you?"

"Absolutely," he responded, without a moment's hesitation. "And we're having some people back to the house afterward for a bite to eat. I hope you both will come for that."

I was stunned. "Are you sure it won't be awkward? Will you have a lot of family around?"

"Well, of course, Lois and Susan will be there."

My heart skipped a beat just hearing him say their names.

"And Julian is flying in this afternoon. I'm going down to Burlington to pick him up. There will be some cousins of Doris's from New York State too."

"How would you introduce me?" I asked cautiously.

"I'll just say you are another cousin," he replied easily. "After all, Julian will be there, and he already knows you."

"That's true," I acknowledged. "In that case, we would love to come. It's very generous of you to invite us. Thank you."

"See you tomorrow, then."

My husband walked into the room just as I put down the phone.

"You won't believe this," I said.

"Try me," he replied. "Nothing can surprise me anymore."

"Bill Horr not only wants us to come to the service, he's also invited us back to the house afterward."

"You have to be kidding."

"No, it's true. I'd fantasized about being asked back afterward and meeting my half-sisters, but even *I* thought that was hoping for too much. Now here is Bill asking us to come over as if it were the most natural thing in the world."

I felt so relieved I couldn't contain myself. Jumping up from the chair, I flung my arms around my husband and hung on tight, feeling his heart beating against me.

"It means everything that we are sharing this together. I'm deeply grateful you were willing to hang in there with me during all those tough times."

He pulled me even closer. "I'm awfully glad we made it."

"All of a sudden I feel scared," I confessed. "The whole idea of sitting in that church tomorrow celebrating my mother's life with no one knowing that I'm her illegitimate daughter feels unnerving and strange. And then I have to lie about who I am to my sisters. I'm not sure I can pull that off when it's such an emotional time for me."

"I know it's going to be tough, but you've gotten this far. I'm sure you'll make it through."

"I just hope you're right."

In the afternoon, I set off by myself across a floating bridge and then climbed up a long hill to a meadow overlooking the town. The tall grasses waving in the breeze looked inviting, and I lay down in them. A blue-winged dragonfly, my favorite insect, darted by. Gazing up at the clouds shape-shifting across the sky, it came to me that I was one with them all. The grass, the clouds, the sky, the dragonfly, and I were all floating in one giant pool together. At the same time, I was being nurtured and held in the arms of Mother Earth. There was no need to worry, no need to try to figure anything out. I only had to trust in the mystery of it all and say yes to life.

*   *   *

That night we both slept badly, rolling around on the lumpy mattress. Waking bleary eyed, the steady drumming of rain on the roof greeted us. Not an auspicious way to start off this momentous day. Bill drove, while I stared in silence at the road ahead, trying to remember to breathe and not give way to panic.

I couldn't help wondering if Bill Horr was already regretting his spontaneous act of inviting us back to the house afterward. And what would it be like when I met my half-sisters?

We arrived in South Hero at 10:25 AM.

"Oh, my God, what will we do for the next half hour?" I asked.

"Let's stop here," said Bill, turning abruptly into the very same apple farm I'd stopped at on my first visit to South Hero.

We went inside, where he proceeded to buy two large bags of crab apples.

"Why on earth are you getting those?"

"I plan to bring them home and make crab apple jelly, of course."

"You mean take them on the plane with us back to Chicago? You must be out of your mind."

"Well, maybe a little," he admitted.

We both started laughing; the air became lighter.

Arriving at the church, I said, "Let's meld in with the others who are walking inside, but first could you pray with me?"

We held hands and asked God to be with us and the rest of the family. A single tear ran down my cheek. It felt good to be in touch with my grief instead of going numb, my usual response.

Inside the church we tried to slip around the people milling about, but a man asked us to sign the guest book. After I wrote our names in an unsteady hand, we sat down in a pew near the back. Behind us, four women were prattling on about everyone who came into the church.

Wouldn't you like to know the identity of the woman sitting right in front of you, I thought. *That would give you something juicy to chew on.*

I was pleased that a good number of people were there to pay their last respects to my mother. Then two men in dark suits came in and took off the white ribbons from the front row. My body started shaking, and I pressed closer to Bill. In walked my two half-sisters, both in blue cotton dresses, their faces stiff with grief. Julian and Bill Horr followed them down the aisle. They all sat down in the pew.

The service began. I tried to pay attention, but it wasn't easy. My eyes kept veering over to the younger-looking of the two women, the only one I could see, who kept wiping her eyes. I remembered that my friend Patty had said before we left for Vermont that maybe my sisters might need me. It was a surprising thought at the time, but perhaps she was right. I began to pray for this half-sister of mine whom it seemed I would never know.

A second minister went up to the pulpit and began speaking about my mother. Some phrases stuck in my mind.

"Doris was quiet and serene," "someone you could never forget," "always congenial and kind," "a true lady."

Then he read a passage in the Bible from Proverbs, which he said perfectly described her:

Who can find a virtuous woman?
For her price is far above rubies....

Listening to his words, I felt deeply moved. Even though I hadn't been able to connect with my mother in this lifetime, in my heart I had always held on to the belief that she was a fine person. Now this tribute to her filled with such praise and respect confirmed to the world the truth that I had known instinctively from the beginning.

When the minister was finished, we sang "Abide with Me" and the service ended. My half-sisters walked back up the aisle, both weeping openly. My heart went out to them.

When it was our turn to leave the pew, I saw that the family was standing in the back of the church greeting everybody. My body stiffened. Even though Bill and I had discussed what we would say in the car coming over, I wasn't certain I was capable of rationally explaining why we were here to my half-sisters, whose feelings of loss I shared.

I found myself standing in front of Bill Horr. He reached out and clasped my outstretched hand in both of his.

"Titia, it's good to see you." His voice broke. Looking me straight in the eye, he added, "Please come over to the house."

I nodded. "Of course we will."

I introduced him to my Bill. Then he turned to his daughters. "Lois, Susan, this is Mr. and Mrs. Ellis. She's a relative of your mother's."

I looked into the tear-stained face of my sister (*Which one did he say this was?*) and murmured something. Then I shook hands with each of them, noting once again that I didn't look like either of them.

Last in line was Julian, looking small and woebegone. I reached out and held his hand. "I'm glad to see you again."

He didn't say anything, but I could see the muscles working in his jaw. His hand clutched mine.

We walked outside, got into our car, and waited for the family to leave. When their car drove off, I said, "Let's stay here a bit until more people go over to the house."

"No," Bill replied, "I think it's better to go now and face it before a lot of people are there."

I felt too weak to argue with him. We arrived just as the four of them were walking down the drive to the house. I made myself get out of the car and smile, trying to act normal, whatever that meant in this unreal situation. Julian and Bill Horr saw us and turned around while the women went on ahead into the house.

We greeted them both, and then Bill excused himself to go in and get things ready. We stayed outside talking with Julian about his recent trip to China. I even asked if he'd mind if my Bill took a picture of him and me, and he agreed.

It was getting colder, and Julian suggested we go inside. My heart began pounding inside my chest. About ten people were standing around chatting. I saw my half-sisters out in the kitchen getting drinks and hurried towards them.

One of them asked what my name was, apologizing that she couldn't remember. I told her and asked which one she was.

"I'm Susan, and this is Lois," she replied, pointing toward her sister, who came over to join us.

"And how are you related to us?" Lois asked.

"I'm a distant cousin of your mother's," I managed to say lightly.

"I could see a resemblance when you were standing next to Uncle Julian outside," Susan observed.

Taken by surprise, I couldn't think of any response.

"How did you find out about the funeral?" Lois wanted to know.

I launched into the story Bill and I had agreed on: that we were visiting his niece who lived in the area, and she had spotted a notice in the local paper about Doris's memorial service. Since we were here anyway, we wanted to pay our respects.

They both nodded and went on with their preparations for lunch.

I felt a little braver now that they had accepted my explanation. "It's been a long time since I saw any of the family," I said casually. "Perhaps you can catch me up on things."

Susan smiled. "You should talk to Uncle Julian about the family history. He's the genealogist."

"I know, but tell me about your life. You're the one in California, aren't you?"

"Yes, I am. I like it out there, but my job is pretty demanding. I'm thinking of moving back here."

"You'd better not," Lois said. "I'm getting tired of my job and was planning to go west."

Just then, Bill Horr appeared at my side. "How do you like my new tie?" he asked. "My neighbor gave it to me for the funeral."

We admired it duly and then chatted about how fortuitous it was that it had stopped raining. Everyone went back out on the sun porch to eat lunch.

I kept my eyes on my sisters. Two more times I followed them into the kitchen to try to make a connection, but each time Bill Horr strode in after me. Was he afraid I might tell them who I was if we were alone together?

Finally, my husband came up to me, pointing to his watch.

"I don't want to cut it too close and miss that plane."

Regretting that we hadn't allowed more time when we changed our reservations, I hesitated, wondering if we should stay longer and try to get on a later plane. But it was obvious my Bill was eager to leave. Equally obvious was the fact that Bill Horr was not going to let me talk alone with his daughters. It must have been a burden for him to keep tabs on me during his time of grief. He had already been more than kind by inviting me into their home. There was nothing more I could do. I walked slowly into the kitchen to say an all-too-brief good-bye to my half-sisters. How I yearned to put my arms around them, but I didn't dare.

Julian and Bill Horr walked out with us. I hugged them both, noticing how old and vulnerable Julian looked. After thanking Bill for inviting us back to the house, we got in our car and pulled out of the driveway. The two men stood there waving us off. They looked forlorn and lost.

When I could see them no longer, I turned to my Bill.

"I still can't believe how all this has worked out. I am incredibly grateful to have been at my mother's memorial service, which really impacted me, especially that final tribute to her. And it was wonderful to meet my half-sisters at long last. What amazing gifts. I should be elated."

"What's wrong?"

"I guess I'm grieving over never having known my mother, and now I will never know my half-sisters either. I was so impressed by those lovely, gracious women who are my flesh-and-blood family. It was more painful than I could have imagined knowing I could never tell them who I am. I can see that telling them the truth right after the memorial service might not have been the best timing, but why not a little later? How I wish Bill Horr could be open to the possibility that Susan and Lois might rejoice in having an older sister, especially since they've just lost their mother."

I sat there lost in thought for a long time.

"I'm not talking about taking her place. No one could ever do that, but I could be a loving presence in their lives, and they in mine. I don't care what anyone says, I believe in my heart our mother would have wanted that."

We were crossing over the causeway from South Hero to the mainland. My heart ached at the thought of losing them now that I had just found them.

"Good-bye, Susan and Lois," I whispered softly as my tears began to fall.

— 17 —

COMING FULL CIRCLE

A FTER MY MOTHER'S MEMORIAL service, my life seemed to have lost its purpose. The dissertation, which I had stopped working on in order to find my mother, lay unheeded on my desk. All I cared about was writing Bill Horr to thank him for his kindness, adding that I would love it if he could send me some photo or keepsake of my mother. When he didn't reply, I was sad but not surprised. His silence said it all.

I no longer had any excuse to keep in contact with my birth mother's family. Only dear Julian kept the lines of correspondence open with his annual Christmas card. Yet I was all too aware that both these men were getting older, and they were the only ones who knew the truth about me. Even if by some wild stroke of fate I ever did get a chance to tell Lois and Susan who I was, there might well be no one left to corroborate my story. But Bill Horr had been so kind and welcoming to me that I didn't feel I had the right to try to persuade him to change his mind.

I would finally hear from Bill over a year later, when he sent me a photo of my mother, sitting in a rocking chair, taken before she became ill. He wrote that not only had Lois gotten married but he was to be married also. I remembered when I was visiting him down in Florida that he had mentioned, almost apologetically, he was seeing a "lady friend." At the time I had encouraged him, saying he needed a life of his own, and he seemed relieved. I wrote back that I was happy for him that he was getting on with his life. At the same time I felt sad that I did not feel I could congratulate my half-sister on her wedding.

My low state of mind back then wasn't helped by my adoptive mother's admission that she was relieved my other mother was dead because now she wouldn't have to worry about my being with her.

A few weeks later when I was coming out of a class at the Family Institute, I ran into Nina Field, an instructor with whom I'd become friends after she had asked me to talk about my search on an adoption panel she had organized. When she inquired how I was doing, I confessed I was sinking.

"I'm free right now," she offered. "Do you want to tell me about it over a cup of coffee?"

Once we were seated in the back of a local café, I brought her up to date.

"I'm wondering if doing this search was worth it," I concluded, shaking my head. "It's turned out to be such a disaster. My birth mother was too senile to connect with. I can't tell my half-sisters who I am, and the man my mother claimed was my father totally denied it. Maybe my adoptive parents are right. Why did I stir up this hornet's nest? I've hurt them and the MacGriffen family, not to mention putting my own marriage at risk by my obsession about this search. Where are the redeeming factors in this picture?"

"Wait a minute," Nina broke in, "you have to distinguish between the outcome and the search itself. What does it say about you that you did this?"

I thought about this for a while.

"It was the first time," I said slowly, "that I ever valued myself enough to pursue a goal that was important just to me. I knew it wouldn't win me love or approval from my adoptive parents and maybe not from the people I contacted." I smiled ruefully, "But I did it."

"What else have you learned?" Nina persisted.

"I'm stronger than I thought I was, and as I think about it, I'm glad I did this search after all. I have found out so much about both my birth parents whose history is my lineage too. Even more, I am realizing as we talk that I found my self."

"Anything else?"

I was silent a long time. Finally I said, "No matter how difficult some of my life has been and occasionally still is with my adoptive parents, I would rather have been raised by them than by my birth mother. This is my path in my present lifetime."

"Tell me more about that," Nina urged.

"When I started to look for my birth mother, I must have hoped on some unconscious level that she would save me. I needed her to give me the love I couldn't give myself and that I didn't feel I got from my adoptive parents. Maybe seeing her again would heal my lifelong wound of feeling I wasn't enough because she gave me up. Not asking for much, was I?

"Then, meeting my half-sisters, it was clear that they struggled just as much as I had when I was in my thirties. But even more I learned there was no guarantee that I would have found greater happiness and fulfillment growing up with my birth mother—especially since she was unmarried—than I would have experienced with my adoptive parents."

I stopped to take in what I had just said.

"Wow, that's quite a revelation, isn't it?"

"It certainly is," Nina said, nodding.

I went on to say that I had fantasized briefly about being brought up by John MacGriffen too, but even though he said he would have raised me if he had been my father (which, of course, he assured me he was not), I knew that wouldn't have worked either. I would have been his illegitimate child, and that was not acceptable in those days.

I stopped to drink some of my coffee and think about all this.

I told her I could see that my search had an unexpected outcome in two ways. Not being able to make meaningful connections with my birth parents pushed me back to my adoptive parents. And even if I had had a successful reunion, I would have needed to be in touch with them often to keep reassuring them that I loved them despite finding my birth parents. What really mattered, I told Nina, was that the more my adoptive parents and I talked, the more honest we were able to be with each other. I not only became more authentic myself, but I began to see each of them as real people with their own wounds and needs.

I added that hearing about my mother's painful childhood with her own mother had helped me understand why it wasn't easy for her to be affectionate with me. When I told my father I was sad we didn't know each other, he had become vulnerable about his blindness and feeling lonely. I wanted to be with him after that and began driving him around town and taking him out to lunch. It brought back the loving feelings I'd had for him as a little child.

I paused for a moment to reflect.

"They weren't perfect parents; neither was I. But I'm learning to love and accept them the way they are. I see that my mother's recent remark about being glad my birth mother was dead was coming out of her fear of losing me. I want to be more empathetic with her instead of taking her words so personally. But the truth is I no longer need to win her affection and approval to feel good about myself."

I stopped and looked over at Nina in surprise. "How freeing that is for me! I'm feeling much better."

"Now it's clear to us both," she said, "why you're glad you were raised by your adoptive parents. Thanks to breaking through all the secrets, you have become your own person—a more difficult task since you were adopted and had to contend with the reality of two sets of parents. By insisting on your right to find your birth mother, you discovered that she and her family were just folks like everyone else. That was the only way you could let go of the fantasy that you would have thrived and been loved unconditionally if you had been raised with them. As a result, you've been able to come to terms with your life with your adoptive parents."

She gave me a big smile. "Good for you."

"But I still have to admit," I said softly, "I would have loved to know my first mother and to have her know me."

"I can understand how you would feel that way."

I sat still for a moment taking in the enormity of what we had discussed. Then I shook off the yearning before it took me over. *Remember,* I told myself, *you can choose your thoughts.*

I turned to my friend and said, "Thanks, Nina. You've helped me see a larger perspective. The first thing I want to do now is go home and finish up my dissertation."

And finish it I did. The following June, Bill and I walked down the aisle together in our caps and gowns to receive our PhDs. It was a great moment.

After my talk with Nina, I had dinner one night with my parents at their home while Bill was out of town. I had been reflecting a great deal about my search and was eager to share my conclusions with them.

When we were all settled in the living room after dinner, enjoying our coffee, I began.

"Once again, I want to let you know where I am in my search."

My parents sat up a little straighter as if bracing themselves for what might be coming next.

I told them that even though the whole process had turned out to be much harder than I ever thought it would be, I felt immensely gratified that I had done it. Despite all the disappointments, I had found my roots on my birth mother's side, and they were admirable ones. I was also in contact with a delightful uncle. All the work I had to do made me a stronger and, I hoped, wiser, more compassionate person.

I stopped for a moment to think about what I wanted to say next.

"But the best and most unexpected outcome is that my search has brought me much closer to both of you. I know it started out being rough and upsetting for us all, but we hung in there and spoke our truth. That resulted in helping me see you both as individuals instead of viewing you only in your roles as my parents. It was wonderful having you visit us in Canada last summer where we could be together in a relaxed atmosphere."

"We certainly enjoyed our time up there," my mother said.

"You were great sports," I told them.

I took a deep breath. There were a few final pieces I wanted to add.

"When it came time to toast you at your fiftieth anniversary in front of all your family and friends, I felt so proud of everything you both have done and who you are. My saying how glad I was that you picked me out was the best way I knew to thank you. That's what this journey of mine has done. It has brought me full circle back to the place of being grateful at a much more profound level that I was adopted and raised by you two."

My mother gasped. "Oh, darling, those words are music to my ears. We are thrilled you feel that way."

"I'm happy too." I smiled over at her. "I really appreciate the remarkable opportunities you have given me over the years, as well as all the doorways that have opened for me as a result of being your daughter.

"One thing in particular that has touched me deeply is your coming to understand and accept that this quest was important to me, whether you agreed with me or not. That's a big part of what I think real love is all about. And I hope you both know how much I love you."

"We feel the same way about you," my mother said, "as well as being immensely proud that you are our daughter."

"I agree," declared my father, as he brushed away the tears from his eyes.

*   *   *

Six years passed. My life was busy and challenging. To our surprise, Bill and I discovered that the time had come to spread our wings and move into Chicago. The hardest part was telling my mother we were leaving. It was especially emotional for her and me since my father was now ill with Alzheimer's disease. At first she was angry and distraught, but to her great credit my mother eventually adjusted with her usual resiliency.

And then a most unexpected thing happened. After we no longer lived next door, I noticed a change occurring between us. My mother seemed to appreciate and respect me more. Perhaps it had something to do with the fact that she could no longer take for granted my being there as her caretaker. And I started seeing her differently too, as an individual in her own right, no longer just locked into her role as my mother whose approval and love I still needed to feel worthwhile. We were now on an equal basis, valuing our mother/daughter relationship, but even more meaningful, moving beyond that to becoming real friends. Who would have guessed that would be one of the outcomes when I set off so many years before on my tumultuous journey?

— 18 —

A SECRET NO LONGER

OPENING MY ANNUAL CHRISTMAS card from Julian Phelps two years later, I was taken aback to read that not only had Bill Horr died but that my half-sister Susan had married and now had a daughter named Christina. I put his card down slowly. Bill dead. My half-sister has a little girl. I have a niece.

My heart gave a leap. With Bill gone, was it possible I could break my promise to their father and contact my half-sisters at long last?

I showed my husband what Julian had written. "I'm thinking of getting in touch with them."

"Are you sure you want to risk it?" he asked.

"I know I'm taking a chance, but what do I have to lose? As it is now, I have no relationship with them anyway. Why wouldn't they like to discover they have a half-sister, especially when they've lost both their parents? But I'm not ready to write them this moment. I'm going to be too busy helping our daughter when she has her baby in a few weeks. That is my most important priority. I'm so excited thinking about our first grandchild coming. Then we'll be moving to Santa Fe in February. My plate is full."

The decision to relocate out west had been a challenging one. I would be ending my career as a therapist just when I felt most fulfilled in that role. In addition, I would be leaving the friends who had stood by me and loved me through all my life changes. Most wrenching, I would be going over a thousand miles away from my mother. She was devastated to hear this news, but having survived our initial move out of her backyard, she resigned herself to the inevitable sooner than I would have expected. We parted from each other with sadness but much love.

I look back now and see that our two years' residence in Chicago was like putting my toe in the water. I was finding out whether I had developed into my own person enough to be able to leave my mother and all that had grounded me throughout my life. The move to Santa Fe, where we knew no one, felt like a big risk but at the same time exhilarating.

We had loved Chicago, but as time passed, we discovered we were not suited for city life. The pace was too fast, and I felt overwhelmed by all the tall buildings, the cement, and the constant noise. I yearned to live closer to the land, drink in the silence, and be surrounded by high mountains, desert grasses, and immense skies filled to overflowing with sunsets that tore my heart open with their beauty.

So many questions were running through me the day we waved good-bye to cherished friends and set off in our car, loaded to the top with all our belongings that didn't make it into the moving van. Who would I be if I were no longer known as a psychologist, or my parents' daughter, or a respected member of the community? What would I do in this strange land? Over the next two days as we drove westward, the words kept coming to me: *Just trust.*

The first week after we arrived in Santa Fe, I was invited by a new friend to attend a writing workshop. It was there I discovered my passion. It seems I had to move far away to a place where I was completely anonymous before I could become free enough to write my story.

For months after we settled into our new home, I struggled over whether to write my half-sisters. Many family members and friends counseled against it, afraid I would come up against one more rejection. In the end I listened to my heart. Despite all my efforts over the years to find my roots, only Julian was left, my once-a-year correspondent. That was not enough to satisfy my longing to know my birth family. Susan and Lois were grown women who had the right to know I existed. They could decide whether they wanted to have a relationship with me or not.

I wrote Julian that I was sorry Bill Horr had died for I knew they had been close. Adding that I was happy to learn about Susan's baby, I admitted that hearing about her had made me long to know my half-sisters. This was a new generation, my generation, and now the next one. I couldn't believe Lois and Susan would think less of their mother for having had me. And they might like to have a new sister. I prayed he would agree. If he did, could he give me their married names and addresses?

He wrote back: "I must respect Bill's wishes. It wouldn't be right for me to let you know where they are unless, of course, you would agree to telling them that you were their second cousin."

Needless to say, I was upset by his answer. No longer was I willing to pretend to be someone's mythical cousin. That would make my whole search a sham. It was time to be honest about who I was. These were my half-sisters. Later that afternoon, I reread the letter and took in for the first time his final sentence. "I wonder if Bill's second wife, Beth, knew about you?"

He included her address and phone number.

Since I never saw Bill or heard from him again after he was married, I had not met Beth. What a surprise that now she was entering into the picture in such an important way.

"Julian does want me to reach them," I told my husband excitedly. "That's why he gave me Beth Horr's address and number. He just can't tell me himself because he'd be going against Bill's wishes. What a canny fellow he is."

I rushed to the phone in the den. Saying a quick prayer, I dialed Beth's number. She answered on the first ring almost as if she had been waiting for my call.

"Mrs. Horr, this is Titia Ellis. You don't know me, but I'm hoping Bill might have told you about me. Julian Phelps gave me your name and phone number."

"Your name isn't familiar," she said warily.

"I have a story to tell you. Do you have time to listen to it?"

"I was just going out, but yes, I'm willing to hear what you have to say."

She didn't speak a word the whole time I talked. I finished by saying, "Even though it pained me to be silent, I've kept my promise to Bill for nine years. Now that he's dead, I believe I have the right to speak my truth. I'm praying, Beth, that you will be willing to help me contact my half-sisters."

There was silence on the other end of the phone. The magnitude of what I was asking for made my heart beat wildly. What would Beth decide?

At last she spoke.

"What an incredible tale. I can't understand why Bill would have wanted to keep your identity a secret from his daughters. Of course, they should know about you. Hold on while I go find their addresses, and good luck."

*   *   *

At last, I could send my half-sisters the letter I had been composing in my heart for so many years. I enclosed a photograph of our family taken a few years back, with all of us seated around our kitchen table. I wished I had one that included our new granddaughter, but this would have to do.

> *Dear Lois and Susan,*
> *I don't know if you remember me, but I met you at*
> *your mother's memorial service in South Hero, where*
> *I was introduced as a second cousin of your mother's.*
> *That was not our real relationship, but it was not the*
> *moment to tell you the truth. I believe in my heart that*
> *now is that time....*

(Here, I told them how it happened that their mother gave birth to me and about my adoptive family. I related the meeting with my mother, which broke my heart because I was too late to connect with her and to thank her with all my heart for giving me life. I described Julian's role of keeping in touch with me over the years, which was how I found out that their father had died and why I'd had to wait this long.)

> *I want you to know I exist because both my*
> *families are an important part of who I am, and you*
> *two are my half-sisters.*

*I realize this will come as an enormous surprise
to you; you may decide you don't want to carry our
relationship any further. But if you are interested in
our getting to know each other better, I would welcome
that. Julian suggested I write to you pretending I was
still that second cousin you were introduced to at the
service. But I am 56 years old and have done a lot of
work on myself in the past 15 years. There is no way I
can do anything except tell you the truth of who I am. I
don't want any more secrets.*

*I'm sure this letter will stir up many questions and
feelings. But eventually I hope we can get to know each
other because I think that at the ages we've all reached,
a secret that was so hurtful to our mother in 1934 can
only be enriching to the three of us now.*

With warm regards,

Titia Ellis

After I mailed off the letters, I wrote Julian telling him what I'd
done and hoping he would understand. The waiting began. I tried to
keep myself busy, but I couldn't stop thinking about what my half-
sisters' reactions might be. Would they want to include me in their
lives? After all, I hadn't had much (let's change that to no) success with
John MacGriffen and his daughter. One thing I already knew was
that I truly liked Susan and Lois since meeting them at our mother's
memorial service.

I didn't have to wait long to find out. Six days later, Susan's letter
arrived.

"This is really amazing and incredibly exciting to find out at this
point in my life that I have a half-sister I didn't know existed before
yesterday. Thank you for enclosing the picture of your family. It helps
make it a little more real. In the photo, your face really reminds me of
Mommy. My husband thinks you resemble Lois."

Soon after, Lois wrote: "You look so much like her. How did we
miss it at the memorial service?"

That was the shock of recognition I had been waiting for all my
life.

Both said that this news didn't make them love their mother any less, that she was the kindest person they had ever known.

Elated by their positive reactions and, of course, thrilled to hear that I looked just like my mother, as well as one of my sisters, I wasted no time in inviting them to visit. Too many years had been lost already. We set a date for October, three months away.

I was being given a second chance to be a sister. Leslie had died fifteen years ago. I had adored her, but our relationship had been complicated due to the differences in our personalities. With Lois and Susan, there was no past history that needed to be explained or forgiven. Since we came from the same lineage, I was certain we were bonded from the beginning.

*   *   *

The sun's last rays were streaking across the sky. I sat on the couch in our new home in Santa Fe, anxiously awaiting the arrival of my new sisters. There was so much on the line. Finding these women was the last piece of my search. If it didn't work out, I would have failed with every significant relationship in my birth family, with the exception of Julian and, of course, Bill Horr, although he wasn't related to me by blood.

The sound of knocking startled me. *Dear God, they are here.* I jumped up and ran to open the door.

There stood two radiant women, one holding a little girl in her arms.

"Welcome," I cried. "You found it. You really are here." The next thing I knew I was hugging them all. Everyone started talking at once.

"Okay," I broke through the din, "I know you are Susan because you are holding Christina and you have the blond hair."

I laughed at the absurdity of not being sure which of my sisters was which.

"That's right," she beamed. She was my height and build and wore jeans just as I did. Her eyes were blue-gray; her long, pale-blond hair was pulled back in a ponytail. Christina was a bubbling one year old, dressed all in pink, with brown hair and beautiful brown eyes.

"And I'm Lois," the other woman stepped forward.

I turned to acknowledge my second sister, who had short brown hair, brown eyes, plus a wide mouth and round face. She too was wearing jeans, and a red suede jacket. I didn't see the likeness to me that Susan had written about, but I focused on the fact that my half-sisters were finally here. That was the most important thing.

All through the afternoon and dinner, we talked, starting the long business of catching up with our lives. After dinner when Christina had been put to bed and Bill had slipped away, we three women sat together on the couch and pored over photo albums, the green one they had brought and our red one.

The next morning, my husband left to go on a fishing trip with a friend. He and I had decided earlier that it would be good for me and my sisters to be alone together for this special time. They turned out to be easy to have around. There was so much we had to tell each other.

Sunday morning we walked down Canyon Road, enjoying the paintings in the galleries and checking out brightly colored quilts, blankets, and silver and turquoise jewelry in the small shops. My friend Patty, who had moved with her husband to Santa Fe shortly after us, was waiting outside one of our favorite restaurants, where she was taking us to lunch.

"I can't believe it!" she exclaimed after I had made the introductions. "It looked as if there were two Titias walking up the street just now. Lois, you two look just alike."

"We do?" we both asked in surprise.

"You mean you can't see it?" Patty was incredulous. "Well, take my word for it."

Before my sisters left, Bill took a photo of the three of us standing outside our home, with the Sangre de Cristo Mountains in the background. Studying that picture later, I had to laugh, as I was able for the first time to see the remarkable resemblance between Lois and me. Our faces were the same round shape, our turned-up noses, wide mouths, and brown eyes identical. Even our hair was cut in the same sporty style. To top it off, her red suede jacket was identical to the blue one I was wearing. After all the years of wondering if there was anyone out there who I looked like in my birth family, the answer had been right in front of me all weekend, and I hadn't even seen it.

The night before my sisters left, we talked about when we would next be together. They had already planned a trip to California the following spring to visit cousins in Los Angeles, see Uncle Julian in Santa Barbara, and then continue driving up the coast.

"Why not come with us and meet all of them?" Susan asked.

I thought about that for a moment. "I'd love to come with you, but how would you introduce me to all those relatives?"

"We could say you're our distant cousin, just as Uncle Julian suggested," Lois said.

"No," I said, "I'm tired of pretending to be someone else."

"You mean you want us to tell everyone who you really are?" Susan asked.

"Why not? After all, whom do we have to protect now? Our mother and your father are dead. You two know who I am, and you've survived the shock."

"We're just sorry we had to wait this long to find out about you," Lois said.

"What's to stop us from telling everyone else in the family the truth?" I asked.

"Nothing," they both said at once.

"I'd like it if you told all the cousins, instead of me. Does that feel all right to you?"

"We'll write out a letter," Susan said, "and show it to you before we send it, and we'll include a photo of the three of us."

"Thank you," I replied gratefully. "It's probably better," I continued, "if you visit the cousins without me. I think my showing up at their doorstep right after they've learned about the daughter Doris gave up for adoption before she was married is pushing it. Some of them may not be as thrilled as you two are with my arrival into the family. I'll meet you afterward in Santa Barbara because I would love to see Julian again and then go from there."

After they left, I wandered around the house. How quiet and empty it felt. I missed the laughter, the talking, the late-night snacks we shared in our bathrobes in front of the fire. I loved these wonderful sisters of mine and felt so blessed to finally have them in my life.

*   *   *

A month later, a copy of my sisters' letter telling the cousins about my existence arrived in the mail.

"We are very pleased to introduce to you, via this letter, your 'new cousin,' our 'new sister,' Titia Ellis. We only learned of her existence ourselves this past summer, and we were all together at her home in Santa Fe, New Mexico, in October, when this picture was taken. It was an amazing and wonderful meeting…"

(They quoted from my first letter to them telling about Doris giving birth to me, my long search to find them, Julian's key role, and describing my adoptive family.)

"Titia is a lovely person. We feel truly blessed to know that we have another sister."

I called each of them to say how deeply moved I was by their warm and loving letter. My sisters' wholehearted acceptance of me filled my heart with immense gratitude. What an antidote to all the long years of rejection and disappointment I had encountered during my search.

$$* \qquad * \qquad *$$

The next April, I flew out to meet Lois, Susan, and Christina in Santa Barbara. I couldn't get over how happy I felt to be with them again. My sisters wasted no time in telling me how excited all the cousins were about my arrival into their family. This good news brought me not only more joy but a great measure of relief as well.

Julian was waiting for us at his retirement community nattily dressed in blue blazer, gray flannels, and striped bow tie.

"So the secret is out," he beamed, giving each of us a little hug.

"And it's thanks to you that we're all together," I replied, looking with affection at this man who had enabled my entry into the Phelps family.

He had aged perceptibly in the years since we had seen each other, but he still had the same twinkle in his eye.

"If you hadn't kept in touch with me all this time, I would never have known that Bill Horr had died. Then you helped me find my sisters in your own clever way."

"I guess you might say I did," Julian chuckled.

Later, back in the car driving up the California coast, I pestered my sisters for stories about our mother.

"Tell me what she loved to do."

"Well, she liked to sew and make things with her hands," Lois said.

"Yes, and she always had a puzzle out on a table for people to work on when they came over," Susan added. "She and Daddy loved to go dancing; they played bridge a lot too."

I had never been into puzzles, but I could relate to going dancing. Bill and I loved doing that when we were younger. As for bridge, I had learned to play at college, but I hadn't cared to since. I had taken a sewing class back then too. The dress I created was a disaster, not fit for any human being to wear.

"I'm not sure we have that much in common," I concluded regretfully.

"You look a lot like her," Lois consoled me.

"And you're so like her in temperament," Susan said. "It's amazing."

"I am?" I perked up. "How?"

"Mommy was so sweet and kind and serene. You are too."

A warning bell went off inside me that triggered a knee-jerk reaction. Momentarily forgetting that I was with my new sisters, I responded from the defensive, wounded part of myself and rejected their kind observations.

"Oh, oh, I don't know if I want to be seen as sweet. It reminds me of how I used to be—trying to meet everyone's needs so they'd love me. That's how I lost myself. When I was doing my search, I had to become strong and stand up to so many people, who didn't think I had the right to know the truth. It has taken long, hard work to become myself."

"We won't call you sweet any longer," Susan quickly replied.

Lois added, "It must have taken such courage to have done this."

"Thank God, I did it," I replied. "It led me to both of you."

*   *   *

Throughout the rest of that year, I received enthusiastic and welcoming letters from my newfound cousins. Some even came by to meet us in Santa Fe as they were touring around the Southwest. Everyone made a point of telling me what a kind, serene person my mother was and that she cherished her family above all else. The ones who met me said I resembled her not only in looks but also in demeanor, the same thing my sisters had pointed out. I was gratified by their words, but aside from looking like her, I couldn't help questioning whether we were really that much alike. Certainly our lifestyles were altogether different. While my birth mother was happily focusing on her daughters, in contrast, the day our youngest son, Frank, entered high school, I was off to graduate school to begin my career as a psychologist. It wasn't that I didn't adore my children—believe me, they were my joy, as well as my greatest teachers! But they were moving out into the world, more involved with peers than parents, and I needed to make a new life of my own.

I certainly didn't feel peaceful during those ensuing years. Being back in school and then starting up a therapy practice took a lot of time, work, and energy. Add to that my quest to find my birth parents moved into high gear, resulting in my becoming totally obsessed. And my jam-packed life didn't stop there.

I became involved with a group called the Ministry of Money who helped me start my first serious philanthropic venture—a family trust in which Bill, our children, and I shared in the decision making for where the money would be contributed. One of the scariest but also most rewarding highlights back then was a trip I made to Calcutta with this group to volunteer with Mother Teresa and the Sisters of Charity in their orphanage and the Home for the Destitute and Dying. Later I co-led a group of people to Haiti where we volunteered with the same order of sisters in Port-au-Prince. I was shaken to my core seeing the abject poverty and countless people dying of HIV/AIDS in this tiny country, only eight hundred miles off our own coast. What struck me most about both these trips was my thinking I had gone there to help people who were suffering. Instead it was those dear women, who had nothing and lay side by side on their cots waiting to die, who poured their love and blessings onto me.

A few years after this, we women formed our own group called Women's Perspective and led workshops that focused on bringing our financial lives into alignment with our core values. We also made trips to Haiti to visit the health clinic we had formed and supported for many years and helped women who had never been able to attend school go to literacy classes.

These experiences strengthened my desire to be out in the world making a difference, in part because I had been so fortunate in my own life and wanted to give something back but even more because I learned so much about what love really was from being with them.

I must admit that when Bill Horr sent me that photo of my birth mother showing her sitting contentedly in her rocking chair knitting, I felt disappointment. That was certainly not how I wanted to be seen.

It was only later I understood that I was judging my mother by my own image of what I considered success to be and what I felt was expected of me. After reflecting deeply on how others had described her, I began to see a loving, devoted wife and mother emerge, who had brought forth two beautiful daughters, placed kindness and her family above accomplishments out in the world, and chosen to live her life in serenity.

I also realized that my birth mother had another side to her that neither of her daughters had known about until I appeared in their midst. I marveled at the bravery she displayed when she risked her future happiness by telling Bill Horr, who had just asked her to marry him, that she had given birth to an illegitimate child and had to relinquish her. I wondered if I would have had the strength to do the same if I'd been in her position.

And thank God she did tell Bill the truth because if he hadn't known about me, I would not have felt I had the right to contact him and reveal her secret. My mother's choice to be honest about her painful past opened the door for me to finally be with her and later to know my half-sisters. I had to think that she must be rejoicing now, knowing that her three daughters were together at last, all because of her daring to tell the truth about her life.

I weep as I write these words because I am seeing that my mother was a person of great courage and integrity, attributes I deeply admire. When she faced the biggest challenges of her young life, she came through with honor. I believe that is key to her being able to attain serenity.

How could I judge this woman who had given me life and created a loving family? I began to think long and hard about the value of kindness and serenity as opposed to striving and accomplishment. I was learning the path to true happiness. At this late date, I was receiving the blessing of my mother's wisdom that I had longed for all along.

And how comforting, if somewhat amazing, to know that even back then it was evident to my sisters that I was my mother's daughter because we had the same nature, despite all my frenzied activity. This was the sense of belonging and sameness and validation for which I had been searching. Now I see those words—"sweet, kind, and serene"—in a new light and gratefully thank my mother for providing me with a way to bring forth these beautiful feminine qualities.

*   *   *

As the correspondence flowed back and forth between the Phelpses and myself, I learned other important information about my mother's family. One letter that really got my attention came from my cousin Patsy.

> "When my eighteen-year old read the letter through,
> her comment was, 'That's beautiful.' I think she could
> particularly relate because she is adopted. We found
> her at an orphanage in South Vietnam when she was
> a baby. Unfortunately, she has virtually no chance
> of ever finding her natural parents with the barrier
> of a foreign country and the fact that the orphanage
> claimed it had no knowledge of who her parents were."

Those words about another adopted person in the family were a real wake-up call for me. I had never known anyone who had been adopted internationally. While I was proclaiming my right to know who I was, insisting that the state laws were wrong to forbid me access to my birth records, this young woman would never be able to find out about her birth parents. It made me realize even more fully how fortunate I was to have been able to locate the information I needed to find my birth family.

An unexpected reaction came from Barton, Julian's younger son.

> Dear Cousin Titia,
> I feel surprised by how wonderfully interesting
> your "arrival" is for me and, I think, for all of us. I
> include my father, the extraordinary secret-keeper, who
> has now expressed great admiration for your diligent
> research.

*My guess is that the Titia letter sent a sort of
unifying spark through a group of people who had
begun to forget each other ...*

The most I ever hoped for in doing this last part of my journey was that my half-sisters and I would end up as friends. It was gratifying to learn that all my work to find my clan had resulted in Julian's affirming my efforts and in the Phelpses' appreciating the importance of family in a fresh way.

Equally important was the fact that any negative reactions to having suddenly acquired a new cousin who was born out of wedlock didn't seem to exist, as least as far as I knew. When I consider that until recently unwed mothers and their offspring have so often been stigmatized and viewed as "less than" throughout our country's history, particularly in the white culture, that spoke volumes to me about the values of my new family. The Phelpses were nonjudgmental, inclusive, and kind, starting with the patriarch, my dear Uncle Julian. How blessed I felt to be welcomed into such a remarkable family.

*   *   *

The following year, Bill and I visited Lois and her husband at their home out in Montana. The first night Lois took me to a meeting of the American Association of University Women. When she introduced me as her sister, the rest of the group laughed and said she didn't have to tell them who I was; it was obvious from just looking at us, that we had to be related. *Yes,* I thought happily, *this is what I've always wanted.*

At Christmas, Lois sent me a beautiful red, green, and purple embroidered belt made by an Afghan women's cooperative. Since I too was concerned for the welfare of women around the world, her gift meant a great deal to me. It still hangs over the chair I sit in as I write.

In January, her husband phoned to tell me that Lois had choked on a piece of meat, gone into a coma, and was in the hospital. I wanted to fly out to be with her, but Bill was seriously ill. I couldn't leave him. Three days later, Susan called in tears to say our sister had died.

I grieved for Lois. It all happened so fast that I couldn't believe she was gone. We were just beginning to know each other, but I had seen the chance for a real friendship with this new sister of mine whom I resembled so closely.

*   *   *

That next summer while Bill and I were up at our camp in Canada, I was dumbfounded to receive a message that Julian Phelps had called. Until I had visited him the year before with my half-sisters, our communication had always been limited to the ritual card at Christmas. He had to have gone to considerable effort to find me. Was something terribly wrong? Bill and I rushed over to the marina so I could call him at the pay phone outside the office. When we were finally connected, I could barely get my breath.

"Julian, are you all right?"

"Oh, I'm fine," he responded jauntily. "My sons and I have been talking about how to celebrate my birthday. So I just wanted to know if you and Bill would be free to come to my eighty-fifth birthday party and family reunion this October?"

"Why, of course," I breathed with a sigh of relief. "We'd love to be there with all of you."

"Good, then we'll go ahead and make our plans. You'll be hearing more from us later."

In October, Bill and I went out to Santa Barbara to join the twenty-five members of the Phelps family who had gathered to celebrate Julian's birthday. I was excited to meet everyone, although I couldn't help wondering if all these new relatives would be as enthusiastic about my unorthodox arrival into the family as the ones I had met so far. It turned out I needn't have worried. I was welcomed with open arms. Everyone exclaimed over how much I looked like my mother and told me how lovely and kind she was.

Upon our arrival we were all presented with garish pink T-shirts, which proclaimed "Julian's 85th" in bold teal letters. I never thought I would want anything to do with a large family group that stood out on account of their matching clothing, constant laughter, and nonstop talking. But when we converged the next morning for breakfast, all sporting our eye-catching shirts, I soon discovered how much I enjoyed being linked to everyone else by this very visible symbol of being part of a clan. I still have that shirt, a reminder of the gathering of my new birth family, which didn't take itself too seriously.

Saturday night, we celebrated Julian's birthday. To my surprise and joy, I was seated at his table. Everyone was invited to share a special memory we had of Julian. When it was my turn, I told the story of my search for my mother and her family starting out with my first phone call to my uncle that morning so many years ago.

"You caught me still in bed," he interrupted, much to everyone's delight.

I laughed too and then related all the ways Julian had helped me during my long journey that led me to be overjoyed to be here with all these wonderful relatives.

At one point during the weekend, Julian invited us all back to his apartment.

"I've been very busy getting ready these past months since we decided to have my birthday celebration," he told us. "The first thing I wanted to do was decorate my rooms. The authorities around here didn't like it, but I told them it's my apartment. I've paid plenty for the privilege of being in it; I can do what I like."

Admiring the feisty nature of my uncle, I shared in the family's amusement.

"Now you can see what I've done," Julian announced as he triumphantly threw open the door to his living room.

What a sight met our eyes. Everywhere were photographs of people and places attached by tape to the walls. Beneath each picture was a piece of white paper identifying the person or the scene above it.

"All these photos are of the Phelps family and where they lived and worked," my uncle announced proudly.

Along with everyone else, I enjoyed going around the rooms peering at photos of people I already knew and others who were slowly becoming familiar. All at once I stopped in front of one particular photograph.

"Why, that's the picture of Lois, Susan, and me taken at our first meeting in Santa Fe."

"Yes," said Julian, suddenly standing at my side, grinning broadly. "I'm glad you sent me a copy of that one. It looks good up there on the wall, wouldn't you say?"

My heart felt so full that I spontaneously flung my arms around this remarkable little man.

"Thank you for everything you've done for me. You are the best uncle I could ever have."

Somehow, seeing that picture up on the wall among all the rest of the Phelps family said it more than anything else. I— Doris's first-born daughter who had been given away for adoption—had finally come home.

— *19* —

MIRACLES ARE POSSIBLE

I HAVE BEEN ON a pilgrimage, discovering more than I ever could have envisioned. And the gifts have continued to unfold. When my daughter and her family surprised us by moving to Vermont, it wasn't long before my inner knowing told me that Bill and I were to follow them. At the very same time Susan and her family relocated to New Hampshire and ended up living only forty minutes away from us. As a result Bill and I were able for the first time to be close to some of our growing family, while Susan and I could rejoice in our sisterhood and create a real friendship. How I love having her as an ongoing part of my life.

Just when I was feeling so thankful for all the gifts that had come my way, life stepped in with two more unexpected blessings. Imagine my astonishment when my daughter Robin, who already had given birth to three children, told me one day while we were on a walk that she and Mark were adopting a child from China. And she added that they were getting a "waiting child"—one with a disability that made his chances of being adopted more difficult. I could hardly believe what I was hearing.

"Tell me more," I begged.

"He's a little boy," Robin said, "one and a half years old, with a cleft lip and palate. He was found lying on the floor in a hospital bathroom with a note on his blanket saying he had been born two days earlier."

She looked over at me, tears in her eyes. "I know a lot of people will think we're crazy."

Was I one of them? They already had three beautiful biological children. What would it be like for this new one to come into an already made family? Would their kids accept him? Would he be able to bond having lived his whole short life in an orphanage? And what would it mean to have been born with this disability? In addition, our daughter and son-in-law were already in their forties. Would they have the energy and dedication required to take on this child who was coming in with such problems?

Thank God my inner knowing told me to voice none of my concerns. Instead I gave her a big hug and out of my heart came the words, "I'm thrilled for you, for us all. And I'll be here for you whenever you need help."

That was also part of the miracle. I literally would be here for her. Oh, the joy of ending up being just a mile away from part of our beloved family. In addition, I was now living in the state where my birth mother and her clan had settled. Who could have ever predicted that I would have ended up here after all the years of my search, which led me to Vermont so long ago?

Even though the process for adopting waiting children was supposed to be facilitated much more quickly because of their special needs, it took a year for my daughter and son-in-law to navigate through all the red tape that was involved. Finally the big day arrived. Robin and Mark had decided to bring their three children with them on this momentous journey. All during that waiting period I wondered how I was going to feel toward this new child. I was used to seeing darling little Chinese girls trotting happily alongside their adoptive parents, but a little boy with a cleft palate (by now doctors in China had fixed his lip) was a whole different scenario. Yet the more Robin showed me new batches of photos from the agency and talked about "Adam," my heart began opening and the concerns melted away. Soon I knew I wanted to be part of the welcoming committee and cautiously inquired if they would mind if I joined them. When they said yes, I was elated.

Arriving in Chengdu exhausted from two days of travel, we were met by Sandy, our guide, who announced we would be going to the orphanage as soon as we left our luggage at the hotel. In the minibus driving over, the immensity of what we were about to do was now upon us. While the children talked excitedly, Mark and Robin sat quietly in front holding hands. When we drove up to the orphanage, we were pleased to see that it was a large new building, light and cheerful. It also contained an immense number of children—from babies up to some that looked to be as old as ten. We were ushered into the waiting room and met the director, who invited us to sit around a large table to await the appearance of our child. Robin was given a sheaf of papers to sign. Each time we heard someone walking down the hall outside, our breath caught in our throats. Finally a young woman came into the room carrying an adorable and very bewildered looking little boy clutching a bottle and a half-eaten candy bar, chocolate smeared all over his face. She popped him into Robin's waiting arms, and everyone finally exhaled.

In that instant all my fears were forgotten as I reveled in the wonder of this child whom my daughter and son-in-law had gone to such lengths to bring into our lives. Even more powerful was the depth of feeling rising up in me. Could I really feel such love for this little being who didn't look or speak like any of us, didn't carry our genes, and came from halfway around the world? My heart answered *yes.*

On the third day, Adam, who had been looking lost and woebegone ever since we took him from the orphanage, delighted us when he suddenly grabbed hold of his new stroller and began to smile as he pushed it all around the hotel lobby. Pretty soon he was laughing as he bumped into chairs or fell over. It was wonderful to see this happy, playful side emerging despite the fact that all he could utter were vowel sounds due to not having a palate.

Soon after we returned to Vermont, Adam underwent a long and difficult operation to create a new palate. For the following ten days, he was encased in casts on his little arms so he wouldn't be able to put his fingers in his mouth and make a hole in the delicate new skin. He never complained, even though he couldn't really understand why this was happening. I sat with him often during this time as we all worked to divert his attention from being so uncomfortable. Soon afterward Adam started speech therapy, and the joy we felt as he laboriously began to sound out words knew no bounds.

By now I had become deeply attached to this beguiling little boy from China, overwhelmed by his courage and sweet disposition. I realized that there was absolutely no difference between the love I felt for Adam and what I felt for all my biological grandchildren. The thought of any difference was "absolutely impossible"—just the words my adoptive mother had written in her fateful letter to me to describe the love she felt for Leslie and me as compared to her love for my brother, Wally, born from her womb. I was so angry at her back then for sending all my identifying information back to the adoption agency that I couldn't believe her words. Now at last I knew that she was speaking the truth from her heart.

A year and a half later, Robin told us they were adopting another waiting child. This time it was a two-year-old girl from Ethiopia who was thought to have a health problem, but she turned out later to be just fine. That December their whole family traveled to Addis Ababa, the capital of Ethiopia, to adopt Tsehay and bring her home with them. Robin told us later about an incident that happened when they arrived back in Boston after forty long hours of travel. Mark and the older children went off to get the car while she waited in Logan Airport with the bags and the two little ones. All at once Tsehay erupted. The exhausting trip and the strangeness of where she was and whom she was with were too much for her. She was inconsolable, crying hysterically and throwing first one shoe and then the other across the floor in desperation. Robin, so tired herself, could find no way to comfort her. She just sat on a duffel bag helplessly watching her new daughter, no doubt questioning how she had ever chosen to get herself in this position.

It was then she felt a tap on her shoulder. A beautiful, dark-skinned couple was standing over her inquiring if this child was from Ethiopia. When she nodded, they smiled. They said they had heard her screams and recognized she was speaking in Amharic, and disclosed that they too were from Ethiopia. They asked if Robin had adopted her. Upon hearing her reply, they thanked her for her generous spirit, told her what a wonderful thing she had done, and said this little girl would have opportunities that never would have been possible for her back in her own country. The man and woman wanted to know if she would mind if they spoke to her daughter. When Robin gratefully assented, they went over to where Tsehay was sobbing, sat down beside her, and began speaking softly to her in Amharic. Soon her tears stopped flowing and a hint of a smile flitted across her face. They picked her up and brought her to Robin, where she settled down into her new mother's lap. Then they retrieved the shoes. At that moment the others returned, and in all the flurry of gathering up luggage and children, Robin never saw the couple again. They disappeared as quietly as they had arrived. I like to think they were guardian angels sent to watch over that family with its priceless treasure from their native land.

*   *   *

What caused our daughter and her husband to adopt these two waiting children from the other side of the world when they already had a wonderful family? I wanted to understand more fully because it seemed as if the answer to this question was tied in some deep way to my own story.

One day at their home while the little ones were taking a nap and the older children were off at school, I posed my question.

Mark spoke up immediately.

"We were living in Los Angeles where I was writing and producing sitcoms, making a lot of money when we started worrying about the values our children were absorbing. It was as if the more they were given, the unhappier they were. We grew anxious about the kind of people they might become. They seemed clueless about how most of the world lived."

"I can understand your concerns," I said, but I couldn't help thinking of how much more aware they were than we had been when we raised our kids in the same affluent suburb in which we had been brought up. It wasn't until our kids were in their teens, and we'd had our midlife crises, that I began thinking about what values and lifestyles were right for me as compared to those of my parents.

I asked if they thought that just moving away from LA would be the answer or if the idea of adopting was being considered back then as well. Robin said that they had vacationed in Vermont a few times and fallen under its spell. So they decided to move there with the hope of simplifying their lives and slowing down the pace of growing up. But they found that the problems followed them.

It was then that they heard about the Fresh Air Fund, which brought inner-city kids out to the country to live with families for two weeks in the summer. They signed up for an eleven-year-old girl, the same age as their daughters. Instead they got Sandor, a six-year-old boy from the Bronx, who had never been away from home before and was very homesick. It was an adjustment shock for everyone that first week, but they all grew to love each other. Now he had been coming for five years. Although their whole family had been sponsoring an assortment of children in a foster parent program for a long time, this marked the next step toward adopting, something they had always thought about on and off.

I wondered aloud if my being adopted had anything to do with that.

"Of course," replied Robin. "The fact that my own mother was adopted—for me it was a lucky thing because it was how we all came to be. That normalizes adoption and makes it a valid way to have our family or to add to it."

"I'm glad of that," I said. My children all knew there had been some difficult issues for me to deal with as an adopted child. Yet Robin had been able to take in what were the underlying good parts of my experience and not be burdened by the rest.

I was sure this had a lot to do with the fact that she and her brothers had always had a close relationship with my adoptive parents, who adored all of them and made it a point to do special trips or outings with each child. I remembered telling my mother once how much I appreciated her being so affirming and affectionate toward our children. Then I couldn't help myself from asking why she hadn't been more like that with me growing up. Instead of becoming defensive, my mother impressed me by saying that she had been brought up by a strict mother and an even tougher nurse who both believed that if a child were praised, she would get a swelled head. She admitted it wasn't until she became a grandmother that she was able to see that probably was not a good way to raise a child. So our children got the best of what my parents could be.

Mark broke into my train of thought and talked about the wild coincidence that my birth mother came from Vermont, which had to mean something. He said that one of the first places they looked at in Vermont was a home in the beautiful town of Newfane where a woman had been running a kind of UN camp for kids from all over the world. They fell in love with that house, and he remembered thinking it would be great to have a lot of children around. Robin added that the old farmhouse they ended up buying also had a lot of room, and they were living in another great town. They asked themselves how they could live there and not adopt.

"It does seem amazing, doesn't it?" I said, shaking my head. " Such an incredible joy for me that you were led to move here to my birth mother's state, and then on top of that you decide to adopt. But what caused you to pick a waiting child?'

Robin said it just happened one day when they were looking up adoption on the Internet and stumbled on a picture of a "waiting child"—a little boy from China with no thumbs and deformed arms.

"I thought, 'Wow, could I do that? Could I adopt a child with those kinds of problems?' Now I know, of course, I can do it. I'd love to do it. We already had three beautiful kids; we didn't need a perfect-looking child."

Mark said they discussed what they were prepared to handle. They lived in rural Vermont where there weren't any facilities for a child who was deaf or blind or who needed some huge heart surgery. Nor did they want to take someone who might be emotionally explosive and disrupt the family such as a child suffering from fetal alcohol syndrome or dreadful abuse. They had had no experience with the cleft world but had heard that it involved a lot of operations. Still it seemed very doable to them in the great scheme of things, as long as one had good health insurance.

"It touches me that you would make this kind of decision," I told them. "I know that in the old days social workers tried to match up adopted children with the family they were going into along religious, ethnic, and socioeconomic backgrounds, even looking for similar traits. I'm glad they did. It made sense in that era when being adopted was not only unusual but also cloaked in secrecy. Many adoptive parents today, as well as their children, still feel more comfortable if it's not physically obvious that their kids are adopted, which I can understand. We all want to 'belong.' But you two have gone just the opposite way and looked for children that not only come from entirely different backgrounds but also have some kind of disability that would make them less likely to be adopted."

Mark said their way made even more sense to them when they were in China and saw all the beautiful little girls in the orphanage. He realized how easily they could walk into a new family, but a waiting child had a much harder time. Kids, who were only three or four, even if there was nothing physically wrong with them, weren't going to be adopted as much because most people wanted a younger child. As a result, they became waiting children even though they were perfectly healthy.

Robin told about how once they narrowed it down, they said they would take the next one that came along, thinking it would be a girl because that was the norm in China. But when the agency sent a photo of a little boy with a cleft lip and palate, it wasn't what they were expecting. Soon after they were sent a picture of a girl with a heart murmur. Then she understood this wasn't like buying a house. They realized if they were sending all these different pictures, the criteria to pick out a child seemed to be which one was cuter. So she decided to approach it as if she were pregnant and take the first child who came their way. That was how they got Adam.

"And you were given a winner," I said, awed by their openness to taking this chance while at the same time marveling that the universe had such a special child in store for them. It just didn't seem like an accident.

My thoughts were confirmed when Mark said, "It's interesting. We couldn't be luckier, but from the reports they sent about Adam, although they were detailed, they didn't describe at all how funny, good-natured, and loving he is, or how brave."

"I don't think they could know," Robin said.

"Probably," he agreed, "but from the description—if I were nervous, there was nothing in there that would have made me pick him out. I think you just have to take a leap of faith."

They talked about deciding that once they adopted Adam, it was clear that they would do it again, and by then they knew waiting children were the only way to go. They also knew they wanted to adopt a girl from Africa next because this continent was hurting and needed help. And the fate of children was awful there, especially for girls.

I asked why they had decided to bring all their children with them both times they adopted.

Acknowledging that it was very unusual, they said how lucky they were that they could afford to do that. Instead of taking their biological children on some cruise or ski vacation, they believed this kind of trip was important to show them what was going on in the "real" world. It also seemed to have helped everyone bond more quickly. As well, adopting these children had had a great effect on their whole family, particularly their oldest daughter. She was going to volunteer with a group of students in Cambodian orphanages in the summer. It had given her a brand new purpose.

So their plan had really worked, I thought. What a courageous and creative way to change everyone's life and values for the better.

When I asked if there was some particular reason why they hadn't adopted domestically, they explained they didn't consider getting a Caucasian child either in this country or abroad because they wanted it to be right out there that they had adopted.

"This kid doesn't look like us. That takes the secretive part out of it from the start."

"I'm right with you there," I said. "That whole secrecy part was such a difficult issue for me growing up. It's hard not to believe that there isn't something awful in your past if everybody is saying you must never know who your birth parents were."

We talked about the fact that they had told the children they were adopted right away. Adam always knew he came from China and that they went over to get him. Tsehay wasn't interested at the moment, even though they often spoke about it with her.

"I know you met her birth mother while you were over there," I said. "It still astounds me and brings tears to my eyes that you did that."

They credited the agency they used for offering that opportunity, which turned out to be the most emotional and important part of their trip. Naturally, they didn't bring Tsehay with them, but all the rest of the family went on the long journey to meet her birth mother.

"I wasn't prepared for the anguish of the mother," Mark said. "She burst into tears when she saw the photos of her daughter that we brought, kissed them several times, and then had to turn away. At that moment I felt the tremendous responsibility of what we were taking on. We have a photo of Robin and the birth mom, arms around each other, their eyes filled with tears. She was a beautiful woman."

Hearing them describe the pain that Tsehay's mother's experienced filled me with sadness for her. The agony of a mother having to give up her child is a universal one. I thought of all the young unmarried women who had been told that relinquishing their children would be best for everyone, that they would forget about their babies and go on with their lives, secure in the knowledge that they had given their child a happy home with two loving parents. But when birth mothers finally began to speak out, it became clear that for the majority, the pain of losing their children still remained. And when older adoptees told their stories, it sometimes turned out that the homes into which they were adopted weren't all that wonderful either.

Robin said that adopting Tsehay was a much more complicated issue than when they got Adam, who was abandoned. Tsehay really had an Ethiopian mother who had to let her daughter go because her only source of income came from selling bananas on a street corner. They were becoming parents for this child in place of her birth mother.

"I was in a relationship with her," Robin said, "which made me realize that she was no different from me, that it's just the luck of how you are born. Why were we lucky and she born so unlucky that she had to give up her daughter? It just doesn't seem fair."

I nodded. She really gets it. She sees that we are all one, that she is no better or different than this other mother. She just happened to be born in the richest country in the world to a mother who just happened to be adopted by parents who could afford to give their child respectability and every material advantage.

Robin added that they wanted to help Tsehay's birth mom but were told that if they sent money, she might be robbed or beaten. In the end they decided to give to an organization that provides aid to poor families in Ethiopia.

Yes, that is the greater plan here, I thought. Having Adam and Tsehay as part of our family hopefully wakes all of us up to the huge inequalities that exist in this world. Like Robin and Mark, we can begin doing something to change this situation. It is not right that mothers are forced to give up their children in order for them to survive and more than that, flourish.

"Anyway, we did the best we could at the time," Robin continued. "We told the birth mother that adoption was part of our family tradition—that my mother was adopted, and so was Adam. And we tried to comfort her, especially when the only thing she asked of us through the translator was if we would send her daughter to school. We promised we'd give her daughter a good education and that we would bring her back to visit when she was older and curious. We'd also let her work or volunteer in Ethiopia if she wants. I would love that. I mean it.

I've learned it's the same as with my biological kids. You just have them for a little while, and then you have to let them go anyway."

I wondered how my daughter had become so wise so young. Letting go was still sometimes an issue for me, especially where my family was concerned.

"Another interesting thing," Mark added, "is that you meet people who are strangers to adoption who ask right out how you can love this adopted kid as much as your blood children."

Whoops. My son-in-law, in his own wonderful, up-front way, had just jumped into the murky waters I had swum in throughout my childhood. I waited to hear his answer.

"Sure," he said, "we've heard of instances where adopted kids arrive having been damaged physically or emotionally or are still grieving the loss of their birth mom, so it's more difficult for everyone to bond. But we were lucky; for us it seemed very easy and instant. Any fears about not having enough love vanished right away. It's actually made our family a much more loving family. I think we were all in a bit of a rut, and it kind of woke everyone up. Our children have become more open hearted and are proud ambassadors for their little brother and sister. And we have all become so comfortable with cleft lip and palate. Now we can see beyond the physical problem to the real person."

"I don't think you have any idea what your words mean to me," I told him, "and what they will mean to others who are adopted. Instead of feeling like we have to work really hard to prove to our parents we are worthy of being adopted (or 'chosen', that word which can have heavy underpinnings), you are turning everything around and saying what a wonderful effect your adopted children have had on your biological family. If all kids who are adopted were told this, they could relax and just be their own persons instead of trying to live up to some impossible ideal the way I felt I had to do."

Mark said that if people were ready to start a family or wanted to add on to an already existing one, he wished they could become aware of all the amazing children out there just waiting for a family and truly understand how great adoption can be.

"I was fortunate enough to have biological children," Robin said, "so I didn't have to fulfill that desire anymore. But I don't personally believe blood is thicker than water. I can love someone just as much who's not connected by blood as those who are. I hear all these people talk about wanting to reproduce their bloodline, but now that I've adopted, I see that Adam is part of our line. So is Tsehay."

"I love your way of putting that," I said. "It shows that families who have adopted kids are inclusive and blessed instead of being less than in some way because they were unable to carry on their genetic line."

"It's bigger even than that," Mark added. "Adopting these children has given us such a renewed purpose in life. You take everything for granted when you're going along having your own kids. When you're adopting, you have to be much more responsible. Before we'd done some silly things in our life, like buying expensive cars and homes. Now our lives have logic and a sense to them. I feel the big picture is there."

Isn't it perfect, I thought, *that Robin and Mark decided to adopt to help their biological children learn better values, and it not only worked beneficially for the kids but for their parents as well, and in the end for us all.*

*　　　　*　　　　*

A year later we talked about adoption again. This time I asked if my search for my birth parents had been an influence on them.

Mark said that there was no question that my story was very much in his unconscious mind when the agency offered them the opportunity to meet with the birth mother, and they immediately said they'd like to do that. He had never forgotten about Corson and Joan sifting through endless pages at the New York Public Library, the eureka moment when they had discovered my name, and my fight against time to meet those people before they died. All that figured greatly in their decision.

Just knowing that they could do away with so much potential sleuthing for Tsehay by meeting her mother made that event the highlight of their trip. It turned out to be a much more profound, ceremonial rite than being handed their new daughter by a woman who was essentially the administrator at the Care Center.

He said his only regret was that they couldn't travel to the birth mother's home, which was two hours south of where they met. Thus they were grateful and touched when their adoption agency made their way to her village earlier and filmed an interview with her mother and uncle, plus took pictures of the hut in which Tsehay had been born. That was his favorite part of the video (which also showed Tsehay growing up in the Care Center in Addis Ababa) and would be incredibly helpful if Tsehay ever decided to find her mother.

Robin added that another profound influence on them, which stemmed directly from my experience, was Adam's story, or nonstory. She said she would always be thankful that their guide, Sandy, took them to the hospital and tracked down the room where they suspected Adam had been left. But they admitted that it would have meant the world to them to have had a glimpse of Adam's mother's or father's face and to be able to tell them how loved their son was.

They both agreed they would help in any way if either of their children decided they wanted to search. The topic was right out there in the open. Adam talked about being adopted all the time. There was a scrapbook filled with photos of when they went to China that he often looked through. It also contained every picture the agency sent before they got him, including before his cleft lip was fixed. As well there was an article that had been placed in the local newspaper, which read, "Abandoned boy left in hospital washroom. Please claim."

"Adam often says he wishes he had been born in my tummy," Robin said. "I used to tell him I wished he had been too, but now I say that I'm glad he was in his other mommy's tummy because she made him who he is, such a wonderful boy, and she gave us an incredible gift."

"He also asks why his mommy didn't keep him, and I tell him that she did the best thing she could do because she probably wasn't able to care for him. But how brave she was."

They acknowledged that Tsehay could long for her birth mother at some deep primal level but that she never mentions her. Robin said she talks about Tsehay's birth mom, but she doesn't push it down her throat. She tells her that they met her mother in Ethiopia. And she has shown her the photo of her mom in the scrapbook. Tsehay isn't interested now, although she is definitely proud of her Ethiopian heritage.

They talked about all the opportunities they were creating for each child to have a connection to their culture and country. They are meeting other Ethiopian families and going to the Ethiopian community to see dances. And Adam, his older brother, and Mark are all taking Chinese lessons.

"I would say you have given these two little ones many wonderful opportunities," I told them.

"We want to," Robin said. "And the other side is that they bring us and everyone else great joy. They pass the love around at their school, and at tennis or ballet. They are like little sponges, eager to soak up whatever new experience comes their way. Adam's speech therapist says he's the highlight of her week. He amazes and delights people. Tsehay's teacher tells me all the time what an impression Tsehay has had on her, that she's so happy and enthusiastic about everything. Now the teacher and her husband are thinking of adopting themselves. That's the kind of effect they have."

*   *   *

Adopting these two children has benefited everyone in our whole family and has inspired other people they meet to think about adopting as well. The way Robin and Mark handle all the issues that were painful for me growing up is totally different and healthy. There are no secrets; everything is out in the open and can be talked about. It is assumed that some day they will want to know more about their past, and the parents will be there to help in any way. But for now Tsehay and Adam know they are loved, and they are blossoming in that love and spreading it around.

I asked my daughter and son-in-law if they had any advice for others who were considering adoption or had already adopted.

Mark said he would tell adoptive parents "to relax and be in the moment. We knew some parents who seem to be always scanning the horizon for signs of trauma, grieving, or loss. Obviously when these problems arise, they need to be dealt with. But for now just love your kids as if you gave birth to them, and the thornier emotional issues you can address later."

Robin added, "I can't tell anyone else what to do. It's very humbling. Kids teach you every day. I know there are some adopted children who have real problems, but biological kids have plenty of struggles too. I can't imagine my life now without them. Adam and Tsehay have changed us for the better in countless ways. I can honestly say it's right up there as one of the best things I have ever done. To find these beings from other countries and then to have them become part of your family makes me believe miracles are possible. Great, mysterious things can happen."

*   *   *

For me these two beautiful additions to our tribe have turned out to be one more confirmation that being loved doesn't depend upon sharing the same bloodline. Because they are so welcomed and adored by everyone with whom they come into contact, I now understand that we are truly all one family, and that our hearts have more love to give than I ever dreamed possible. I talk with Adam and Tsehay about my being adopted too and tell them that we share losses but also great gifts. They in turn teach me to be more playful by inviting me to join them in their uninhibited dances where we dress up in veils and outlandish hats and end up rolling on the floor in helpless fits of laughter. Thanks to them, I am rediscovering my own long buried free spirited child. Seeing all the spontaneous blessings they bring to our family and to the larger family shows me that I too brought gifts to my family, as does every child, whether biological or adopted.

This is a story about moving from fear to love. I began life feeling unlovable and frightened because I had lost the mother who had nurtured me in her womb for nine months. Since this wound occurred before I could comprehend or speak, I had no way to express my grief. I only was aware of a hole inside me, which I endeavored to fill by trying to please others so they would never leave me. This required that I abandon my true self.

In mid-life I embarked on a search for my birth mother with the hope that she would heal me. When she was unable to be there for me on the physical plane, I realized, with much spiritual and psychological help, that *I* needed to give my self the nurturing I had wanted from her. I discovered I had erected a wall around my heart, which kept me from freely showing affection to people out of fear that I might lose them. The wall also fended off the love offered me by others. Because I had so little regard for my self, I didn't believe anyone else could care for me either. During my healing process I began to accept and then to love all the disparate pieces of my life and of my self. It was then that a wellspring of gratitude flowed in to replace that wall.

Many mystical experiences occurred along my journey. Although not available in body and mind, my birth mother visited me on the spiritual realm. The two meetings I had with her, one out on her deck and the other down at the lake, filled me with her everlasting love. Some of you may have trouble believing that these and other events I describe really happened. But if my story has touched you in any way, why not dare to be open to the mysterious forces that are waiting to unfold in your life? Ask your heart what it most desires, speak your truth, and be open to whatever outcome appears. Goethe spoke of the magic that follows as Providence, but there are many terms: Mother Nature, God, Buddha, the Great Spirit, and the universe. The list goes on; the names don't really matter. In the end they all mean Love.

— 20 —

WHAT WE CAN DO

A s someone who was also given up and then adopted by a loving family, I am especially grateful that Tsehay and Adam will not have to remain in their orphanages being those waiting children all their lives. But then I think about how many children around the world suffer this fate or worse.

The *New York Times* did a series of articles about the tragic condition of children in Africa. There was a poignant picture on the front page of a six-year-old boy (just Adam's age) who had been sold to a fisherman by his desperately poor parents. This little child, who had no idea how to swim, was forced to go out all day in a small boat, risking his life to help the man catch fish. Reading his story broke my heart. I woke up one night haunted by his face and the faces of a multitude of other starving, diseased, orphaned children in the world.

How could I be of help? Immediately the knowing came to me to start a fund for children in need and that the royalties from selling my book could fuel it. Then came the reality check—reminding me that only best-sellers make a lot of money. However, since Bill and I had been talking about wanting to simplify our life, maybe this was the right moment to put our home on the market.

Nine months later, the house was sold, and the All One Family Fund was born from the proceeds. The mission of the Fund is to help children thrive by creating healthy family situations for orphans and those at risk. This is done by partnering with already existing organizations to provide health, safety, and support for vulnerable children and families, particularly where drugs, HIV/AIDS, war, and genocide have decimated the adult population. The work is carried out in tandem with local communities who understand best the needs of their children and caretakers.

We can no longer rely on overburdened governments to support children and families in need. Philanthropists, a beautiful word from the Greeks meaning friends or lovers of humankind, such as Bill and Melinda Gates are leading the way to find solutions to the crises facing children in our world. But every one of us can be a philanthropist by donating any amount of money and/or contributing time and energy to this vital cause. I become excited and hopeful as I envision us partnering together in this great venture, inspired by our realization that all children are our children.

Perhaps you are considering adopting a child internationally or domestically. There are also roughly 125,000 children in foster care programs in this country who are available for adoption. From observing my daughter and son-in-law's experience, I have learned how important it was for them to go through a reputable agency that offered both pre- and post-adoption services. If you decide to take this leap of faith, your action can lead to unexpected blessings. And yes, there will also be challenges, but show me a family who doesn't have these.

There are also other avenues available to help the children. A wonderful way to start is simply to notice if there is any child around you who needs love and find ways to be there for him or her. You might also want to give to the All One Family Fund. Or you may feel you want to start your own fund with some of your family or friends or just donate directly to a charity that touches your heart. Many organizations offer the opportunity to sponsor an at-risk child, which could involve sending a monthly sum of money and/or writing letters, exchanging photos, and encouraging them to attend school. That has been a meaningful path for Bill and me to connect with children over the years.

Now with this new Fund, we can help in other ways. My granddaughter Rosie (Robin and Mark's oldest child) and I had the privilege recently of visiting three of the organizations we are helping to support in Africa. I needed to go first to Ethiopia to see the people and the land from which Tsehay, our amazing granddaughter, had come.

While we were in Addis Ababa, we visited the Care Center sponsored by the Children Home Society and Family Services in St. Paul, Minnesota, the agency that helped Robin and Mark adopt Tsehay. What I admire about this particular group is that they have always focused first on ways to help families stay together whenever possible, instead of offering parents no choice but to give their children up for adoption. The agency does this by working to build stronger communities, which provide vital services such as schools, health care, and jobs so that everyone receives the help they need. After we distributed a supply of diapers and children's books, we spent the afternoon with the staff, some of whom remembered Tsehay, and played with the babies and small children. When it was time to leave, Rosie was all ready to adopt a sweet little boy who had completely won her heart.

Later we flew to Rwanda, a beautiful country, where the horrors of the genocide are still very much in evidence. There we met with the staff of CHABHA (Children Affected by HIV/AIDS) who were grateful for the duffel bag of books we had brought over in response to the children's desire to learn English so they might obtain better jobs. One of the events they arranged for us to attend was a gathering of about four hundred youngsters, all stricken with HIV/AIDS and orphaned during the genocide. They come together one afternoon a week under the leadership of enthusiastic, caring young adults, many of whom are also orphaned and living with HIV/AIDS, to play games, sing, dance, and hear inspiring messages to help them forget for a short time the traumas they have been through and continue to endure.

Another day we drove out into the country to visit a once abandoned hospital, now completely restored and equipped with the latest medical technology by Partners in Health (started by Dr. Paul Farmer). It also has a new clinic and organic gardens to serve the needs of families in the area. The dedication and optimism of the staff whom we met here and at the other organizations we visited left us feeling grateful in the knowledge that the groups we were supporting were making a visible difference.

My deepest wish is that people will choose to react with love and hope instead of becoming overwhelmed by all the bad news in the world. The power for good that can be unleashed when we come together committed to cherishing the children is a mighty force. The best part is that everyone benefits. I know from my own experience that once we become involved with these young ones, the joy that flows back into our hearts and lives will be more than we can imagine.

GREAT BLESSINGS & LOVE

TO EACH OF YOU

Appendix

Visit my website at www.titiaellis.com to find out more about *The Search*, the author, and updates on adoption and related issues.

The Search can be ordered directly from the website or on Amazon.com or www.barnesandnoble.com. All proceeds from the sale of the books will go to the All One Family Fund.

Information about the All One Family Fund can be found at www.titiaellis.com or www.allonefamilyfund.org.

Donations to the All One Family Fund can be made on the website or by sending a check payable to:

All One Family Fund/Triskeles Foundation (all on one line)
c/o Triskeles Foundation
    707 Eagleview Blvd., Suite 105
    Exton, PA 19341
    Phone: 610-321-9876
    website: www.triskeles.org

ALL ONE FAMILY FUND

Mission Statement

To integrate at-risk children into healthy family situations.

Strategies

All One Family Fund cooperates with local communities, who best understand the needs of their children and caregivers.

We partner with nonprofit organizations to support vulnerable families and, when appropriate, to facilitate adoptions for orphans and children in foster care.

We assist the work of those who innovate new kinds of families, particularly where HIV/AIDS, genocide, or war have decimated the adult population.

Information

For more information about the Fund, please visit our Web site: www.allonefamilyfund.org

ALL ONE FAMILY FUND Grant Recipients

Central Asia Institute (building schools for girls in Pakistan and Afghanistan, founded by Greg Mortenson, author of *Three Cups of Tea*)

CHABHA (working with local communities to support orphans affected by HIV/AIDS in Rwanda)

Children's Home Society & Family Services (providing domestic and international adoption services, plus supporting family development programs in Addis Ababa & Hossana, Ethiopia)

Doctors without Borders (providing care for women and children in refugee camps in Darfur)

Indian River County, Florida Healthy Start Coalition, Inc. (providing services during pregnancy and through the earliest stages of a child's life)

Firelight Foundation (supporting local community groups helping children and families affected by HIV/AIDS and poverty in Sub-Saharan Africa)

Fonkoze USA (providing micro loans to vulnerable women in Haiti)

Friends of African Village Libraries (helping children in African villages read)

Friends without Borders (supporting Angkor Hospital, which provides free medical care to children and training of medical personnel in Cambodia)

Garrison Forest School (scholarship fund for girls)

Haiti Partners (creating schools and training teachers for children in Haiti)

Life and Hope Association (orphanage in Cambodia with a special project that educates girls and teaches job skills)

Ms. Foundation (providing health protection for girls in the U.S. and promoting family planning)

Nepalese Youth Opportunity Foundation (freeing young girls from indentured servitude in Western Nepal)

Old Dog Documentaries, Grandmother to Grandmother (two projects—one in the Bronx, one in Tanzania—supporting grandmothers who are raising grandchildren)

Partners in Health (supporting a unique model of total health care, created by Dr. Paul Farmer, for at-risk families in Haiti, Rwanda, and other countries)

Planned Parenthood Northern New England (providing health protection for young people and promoting family planning)

Santa Fe Mountain Center (helping underserved youth, adults, and communities realize their potential)

Smile Train (providing free surgery for children with cleft lip and palate and training local doctors)

Spence Chapin (providing adoption services domestically and internationally)

STRIVE (providing job training and ongoing job support for at-risk youth and adults in Boston area)

Tanzanian Children's Fund (working with local communities to provide housing, health, and educational support for children in need)

The Family Institute at Northwestern University (providing counseling for families with adoption issues and training health workers specializing in this field)

The Upper Valley Haven (providing shelter and services for homeless families in Vermont and New Hampshire)

Woodstock Community Food Shelf (providing food for people in need around the Woodstock, Vermont, area)

Recommended Books and Films

A Love Like No Other: Stories From Adoptive Parents, Edited by Pamela Kruger and Jill Smolowe (Riverhead Books, New York 2005)

Adoption Healing...A Path to Recovery by Joe Soll, CSW (Gateway Press, Baltimore, MD 2000)

Adoption Nation: How the Adoption Revolution Is Transforming America by Adam Pertman (Basic Books, Perseus Books Group 2000)

An Intimate Journey into the Heart of Adoption by Lynn C. Franklin with Elizabeth Ferber (Harmony Books, New York 1998)

Being Adopted: The Lifelong Search for Self by David M. Brodzinsky, PhD, Marshall D. Schechter, MD, and Robin Marantz Henig (First Anchor Books 1993)

Children of Open Adoption and Their Families by Kathleen Silber and Patricia Martinez Dorner (Corona Publishing, San Antonio, TX 1990)

Coming Home to Self: The Adopted Child Grows Up by Nancy Newton Verrier (Gateway Press, Inc. Baltimore, MD 2003)

Family Matters: Secrecy and Disclosure in the History of Adoption by E. Wayne Carp (First Harvard University Press 2000)

Ithaka: A Daughter's Memoir of Being Found by Sarah Saffian (Delta Books 1999)

Journey of the Adopted Self: A Quest for Wholeness by Betty Jean Lifton (Basic Books, HarperCollins 1994)

Nurturing Adoptions: Creating Resilience after Neglect and Trauma by Deborah D. Gray (Perspective Press, Indianapolis, IN 2007)

Raising Adopted Children: Practical Reassuring Advice for Every Adoptive Parent by Lois Ruskai Melina (Quill, HarperCollins, New York, Revised Edition 2002)

Stories of Adoption by Eric Blau (New Sage Press, Portland, OR 1993)

The Adoption Triangle: The Effects of the Sealed Record on Adoptees, Birth Parents and Adoptive Parents by Arthur D. Sorosky, MD, Annette Baran, MSW, Reuben Pannor, MSW (Anchor Press, Doubleday, Garden City, New York 1979)

The Other Mother by Carol Schaefer (Soho Press,Inc., New York, 1991)

The Girls Who Went Away: The Hidden History of Women Who Surrendered Children for Adoption in the Decades Before Roe V. Wade by Ann Fessler (Penguin Press, New York 2006)

The Primal Wound: Understanding the Adopted Child by Nancy Newton Verrier (Gateway Press, Baltimore 1993)

The Search for Anna Fisher by Florence Fisher (Published by Fawcett Books, CBS Publications 1973)

Toddler Adoption: The Weaver's Craft by Mary Hopkins-Best (Perspectives Press, Indianapolis, IN 1997)

Twenty Things Adopted Kids Wish Their Adoptive Parents Knew by Sherrie Eldridge (Published by Bantam Dell, Random House 1999)

Twice Born: Memoirs of an Adopted Daughter by Betty Jean Lifton (Penguin Books, England 1975)

Children's Books

All About Adoption: How Families Are Made and How Kids Feel About It by Marc Nemiroff and Jane Annunziata, illustrated by Carol Koeller (Magination Press, Washington DC 2004)

I Love You Like Crazy Cakes by Rose A. Lewis and Jane Dyer, illustrator (Little Brown 2000)—the story of a little girl adopted from China

The Red Blanket by Eliza Thomas and Joe Cepeda, illustrator (Hachette Book Group 2004)—the story of a little boy adopted from China

The Runaway Bunny by Margaret Wise Brown and Clement Hurd, illustrator (PG, HarperCollins Children 2005)—a classic tale for all children about a mother's love for her child

We Belong Together: A Book about Adoption and Families by Todd Parr (Little Brown, New York 2007)

Three Cups of Tea: One Man's Journey to Change the World ...One Child at a Time by Greg Mortenson, The Young Reader's Edition, adapted by Sarah Thomson with foreword by Jane Goodall (Puffin Books, Penguin Group, New York 2009)

Listen to the Wind: The Story of Dr. Greg and Three Cups of Tea by Greg Mortenson with Susan L. Roth, illustrations by Susan L. Roth (Dal Books for Young Readers, Penguin Young Readers Group, New York 2009)

Novels

The Cider House Rules by John Irving (William Morris 1985)— life in an orphanage in the first half of the twentieth century in rural Maine, founded and run by a doctor, and his favorite orphan

The Cradle by Patrick Somerville (Little Brown, New York 2009)—a husband goes on a journey to find the cradle his pregnant wife slept in as a baby

The Patron Saint of Liars by Ann Patchett (Harper Collins 1992)—a young pregnant woman goes to a "home," where she gives birth to a daughter and makes a life-changing decision

Then She Found Me by Elinor Lipman (Pocket Books, Simon & Schuster 1990)—an adopted woman is found by her birth mother. Funny and poignant

Inspirational Books

Finding Beauty in a Broken World by Terry Tempest Williams (Vintage Books, Random House, New York. 2009)—author describes a visit to Rwanda to help create a memorial for those killed in the genocide

Half the Sky: Turning Oppression into Opportunity for Women Worldwide by Nicholas D. Kristoff and Sheryl WuDunn (Knopf, New York 2009)

Inspired Philanthropy: Your Step-by-Step Guide to Creating a Giving Plan and Leaving a Legacy by Tracy Gary, Kim Klein, Suze Orman, and Nancy Adess (Kim Klein's Chardon Press, 2007)

The Power of Giving: How Giving Back Enriches Us All by Azim Jamal and Harvey McKinnon (Jeremy P. Tarcher, Penguin, New York 2008)

Mountains Beyond Mountains: The Quest of Dr. Paul Farmer, A Man

Who Would Cure the World by Tracy Kidder (Random House, New York 2003)

Stones into Schools: Promoting Peace with Books, Not Bombs, in Afghanistan and Pakistan by Greg Mortenson (Viking, Penguin Group, New York 2009)

There Is No Me Without You: One Woman's Odyssey to Rescue Africa's Children by Melissa Fay Greene (Bloomsbury, New York 2006)

Three Cups of Tea: One Man's Journey to Change the World ...One Child at a Time by Greg Mortenson (Viking, Penguin Group, New York 2006)

Films

Daughter of Keltoum. An Algerian film by Mehdi Charef—a young Swiss woman travels to her birthplace, an isolated, barren Berber settlement in a mountainous desert landscape, to find her birth mother

Secrets and Lies. A United Kingdom film by Mike Leigh—an unmarried woman living a difficult life in the ragged outskirts of London is found by the daughter she relinquished at birth

The Cider House Rules. A U.S. film 1999. Directed by Lasse Hallstrom, based on the novel *The Cider House Rules* by John Irving—depicts life in an orphanage in the mid-1900s, created and run by Dr. Larch, and his favorite orphan, Homer Wells

Documentaries

Grandmother to Grandmother: New York to Tanzania created 2009 by Old Dog Documentaries, directed by Anne Macksoud and John Ankele—two projects, in the Bronx and in Tanzania, are finding ways to support grandmothers raising grandchildren whose parents are either dead from AIDS in Africa or wiped out from AIDS, drugs, and violence in cities across America

Smile Pinki. The 2008 winner of the Academy Award for Best Short Documentary, directed by Megan Mylan, made in Hindi and Bhopuri—a poor girl in rural India has her life transformed when she receives surgery to correct her cleft lip, thanks to the Smile Train

About the Author

Born in New York City, Titia Ellis was adopted and then raised outside of Chicago. Trained as a psychologist, she maintained a family therapy practice for many years. Titia and her husband, Bill, founded the All One Family Fund in 2008 to help children at risk. They live in Vermont and delight in visits with their three children and nine grandchildren.

Manufactured By: RR Donnelley
Breinigsville, PA USA
December, 2010